anna getty's
Easy Green Organic

anna getty's
Easy Green Organic

cook well–eat well–live well

PHOTOGRAPHS BY
DAN GOLDBERG AND RON HAMAD

CHRONICLE BOOKS

SAN FRANCISCO

Library of Congress Cataloging-in-Publication Data:
Getty, Anna.
    Anna Getty's easy green organic : cook well, eat well, live well / photographs by
Dan Goldberg and Ron Hamad.
        p. cm.
    Includes index.
    ISBN 978-0-8118-6668-2 (pbk.)
1. Cookery (Natural foods) I. Title. II. Title: Easy green organic.
    TX741.G48 2009

Manufactured in China.

Designed by Anne Donnard
Prop styling by Kami Bremyer
Food styling by Erin Quon
Typesetting by DC Typography, San Francisco.

The photographers wish to thank Alex Marshall Studios, Heath Ceramics, Laura Newlin/Sausalito Pottery, and Soule Studio for graciously lending us props for the photographs.

10 9 8 7 6 5 4 3 2 1

Chronicle Books LLC
680 Second Street
San Francisco, California 94107

www.chroniclebooks.com

To my husband, who tells me all the time how much he loves the food I cook. Thank you for your loving support.

To my daughter, for inspiring me every day.

ACKNOWLEDGMENTS

Thank you:

To Mom, despite your reluctance to be in the kitchen, I have learned so much about food and cooking from you.

To Oma Gail, you gave me my first real set of pots and pans.

To all my family members for being on this great ride of life with me.

To Darra Crouch for hiring me with so little experience and forgiving me when I burned the salmon. Hadley, you introduced me to Darra in the first place. You are a true good friend to me. We will always have the mashed potatoes on the face night.

To Alex, another amazing cook.

To Akasha, my dear friend and organic food mentor. You always told me I was a good "seasoner." And thank you for letting us shoot photos in your amazing restaurant Akasha. I am so proud of you.

To Alisa, my dear, dear friend and backbone in this endeavor and others.

To Rob Weller, Gary Grossman, and Debbie Supnik. Wasn't the cookbook your idea in the first place? You have all been my cheerleaders.

To my faithful recipe developers Amy Brown, Paul Barnet, and JJ. You all kept my spirits high in the kitchen while lending me your distinguished palates and skills.

To all my friends who came by day after day for "tastings."

And to all my friends who have supported me along the way. Jeff Vespa, always there to push me in great ways; Debbie de la B., for your love and never-ending encouragement; Sat Kaur, for lending me your husband in the kitchen and for your love and support; Laura Holmes Haddad, for your expertise and for really saving the day.

To my photographers Dan Goldberg and Ron Hamad and the entire team who helped make this book so beautiful.

To Bill LeBlond, Sarah Billingsley, Doug Ogan, Anne Donnard, Jane Chinn, and the Chronicle team. It has been a great honor working with you.

To the Organic Center for your support and the great work you do.

To all the farmers who strive to bring us organic food that is as pure as nature intended.

To all the chefs who inspire me.

To Gahl, the astrologer, you always told me I was "meant to write." Your words have guided me and continue to do so.

To all the leaders in the health and sustainability movement. We still have a long way to go to help this planet heal but because of all of you, I am optimistic.

To Justin Meyers, Paul Knobel, and my Sutton Place team, thank you all. You always have my back.

To Matthew Guma.

To David Silverman. Thank you for the second kitchen.

To Nina and Jessica for recipe logging. You rock.

To Dan and Hal. You're the best.

To all my friends who came by day after day for "tastings," Amy S., Hartwell, and Juliet R.

Thank you Dr. Alan Greene and Cheryl Greene for your never-ending support. You inspire me . . . and for loaning an excerpt from *Raising Baby Green* to this book.

Thank you Green Gulch and Tassajara for my roots.

Thank you to the farmers at Hollywood Farmers market, especially Julian and Carol Pearce at Soledad Goats, Laura my avocado gal, and the "Jazzy Sproutman."

contents

preface

I was born in Germany and raised in both Los Angeles and San Francisco. My mother, Gisela, studied Buddhism in the early 1980s at the Green Gulch Center in Marin County, California. And that is where my food education began. I watched Buddhist monks lovingly farm organic fruits and vegetables, which made their way across the Golden Gate Bridge to the famous vegetarian restaurant, Greens, which we frequented. We were strictly vegetarian at the time—and I mean *really* vegetarian. I remember going into our small local health food store and slicing chunks of milky-white tofu from large slabs floating in tubs of water. (It sounds really appetizing, right?)

I grew up eating lentil soup, whole-wheat pasta, and nutritional yeast flakes when those ingredients were virtually unheard of in most American households. We had a lovely little garden at our house, and my mother cut fresh herbs, which she added to our soups and salads. That was the extent of the cuisine in our home: no homemade cookies or pies, no casseroles like macaroni and cheese. I didn't appreciate the simplicity of our food and, as a kid, I may have even thought it disgusting at times. But looking back now I realize our meals were simple, fresh, locally harvested, seasonal, and very flavorful—exactly the way food should be.

I have spent much of my life traveling and enjoying flavors and dishes from all over the world. Even now, my husband, daughter, and I feel blessed that our families are spread out across both America and Europe. Whether we're in Chicago for Thanksgiving, in the English countryside for Christmas, or in Italy for whatever reason we can find, I'm always on the lookout for new healthful, satisfying food experiences.

That's not to say it has always been this way. When I moved to Paris to attend college, all I knew how to make were scrambled eggs, ramen noodles, my grandmother's easy pasta sauce, and a cup of coffee. Like Julia Child, I refined my palate in France. However, Julia gained culinary expertise while I gained weight and only a smattering of kitchen skills. But I also gained an appreciation for fresh food. I started enjoying the benefits of the neighborhood farmers' markets and the vast array of fresh and local produce that is commonplace in Paris, a food lover's paradise. As I became more comfortable with the language and my neighborhood, I also became more comfortable in the kitchen and tried my hand at soups, quiches, sauces, and dressings.

After three years in Paris, I returned home to Los Angeles in desperate need of a job. This is not the best way to show up in any city, particularly L.A. As great as it is—and it is a truly wonderful city—L.A. can be a very unforgiving environment if you don't have a car or a sense of direction. (And I mean that geographically as well as in reference to life choices.)

In 1995, one of my best girlfriends told me her catering boss needed someone to help in the kitchen and I jumped at the opportunity. Although I knew how to hold a knife correctly and could tell a shallot from a garlic bulb, I was not especially qualified to be an assistant to a professional caterer (a Hollywood caterer, no less). But I had a great attitude, was willing to work with people, and truly wanted to learn how to cook.

This passion to learn was so strong that I worked in catering on and off for seven years, gaining a lot of experience, allies, and one significant life-changing friend: One of my employers, Akasha Richmond—known as "the chef to the stars"—reintroduced me to organic food and simple, pure ingredients with great joy and passion. It was through her enthusiasm that I became reacquainted with the uncomplicated, beautiful ingredients of my childhood. My catering days began more than a decade ago, and my love affair with organic food and cooking has been growing every day.

My relationship with Akasha led me to the Organic Center. The center is a nonprofit organization that conducts peer-reviewed scientific research and presents factual evidence on why organic food is better for our health and the health of the planet. Learning about their work was a real awakening for me. I decided I wanted to be of service by spreading their message about the healing qualities of all things organic.

For the past few years I have been working with and supporting the Organic Center and other organizations, such as Healthy Child Healthy World and the Organic Farming Research Foundation. In the process, I have educated myself about organic and sustainably produced food, and an overall green and sustainable lifestyle. I felt there was more to organic cooking than buying green and eco-friendly ingredients. I have also been striving to eliminate toxins from my home environment. Becoming a mother has made me even more particular about the products I bring into my house for my family, particularly food.

I believe we can initiate change in myriad ways, including through our purchasing power, which we exercise when choosing the food we eat and the products we use. We can choose to be conscientious and responsible consumers. If we demand organic food and goods, over time the supply will expand to meet our demand. We can make positive changes in the food industry and for the environment simply by the way we choose to live our day-to-day lives.

It is our responsibility to continue educating ourselves in ways that enhance healthful diets, fit bodies, and a healthy planet. And I mean that we must do this actively through the Internet and reading books, through getting to know the managers at our local grocery stores or the farmers at our local farmers' markets. Another really great way to learn more about organic food is to grow some. A small organic garden, a kitchen herb box, or even one small pot of basil or rosemary helps improve your food awareness by affirming your connection to the natural growing process. I believe these simple actions can help create a ripple effect in our collective awareness of food and nutrition. At the very least, they will benefit us individually, which is reason enough to participate.

I'm reminded of a quote by Carl Jung: "Every person needs to have a piece of garden, however small, to keep them in touch with the earth and therefore with something deeper in themselves."

Reconnect to food and its power to nourish your mind, body, and spirit. Empower yourself through your kitchen and the food you prepare. And most important, take baby steps. I realize the idea of going green and organic may seem daunting, but know you have the resources to guide you along the way. To kick-start this organic education, I have asked the Organic Center to contribute their expertise to this book. I cannot extend my gratitude enough to them for their support of this project. Please enjoy the fun fact boxes, which contain some of the Organic Center's data, I have scattered throughout the book.

I love to cook and have learned over the years to develop a close and conscious relationship to food and where it comes from. It is my goal to share this love and enthusiasm with you. Most of the recipes are quick and uncomplicated, but more important, they are delicious. Like the title says, they are easy, green, and organic. Welcome to my kitchen!

> "It is vitally important that we can continue to say, with absolute conviction, that organic farming delivers the highest quality, best-tasting food, produced without artificial chemicals or genetic modification, and with respect for animal welfare and the environment, while helping to maintain the landscape and rural communities." —*Prince Charles*

Never have the topics of green, organic, and sustainable agriculture been more popular in the modern Western world than they are now. With the realities of global warming and the stark depletion of the earth's resources, such as water, coal, oil, and natural gas, people are beginning to realize that we must make a change; our planet's survival depends on it. We must not only educate ourselves about what it means to live sustainably, but also expand our awareness of the consequences of our current course. Consider, for instance, that almost every other species would benefit from the extinction of ours. Can we humans release ourselves from our narcissistic assumption that we are more important than all other life forms, so that we might see ourselves as one species among many? Ought we not to at least try to exchange some of our control *over* nature and recognize our interdependence *with* it?

Don't worry, I'm not going to jump up on an (organic) apple crate and go off on some kind of eco-maniacal rant. None of us responds well to lectures, however well intended they may be. But it seems rather obvious that so many of us have lost our connection to the food we put into our bodies. Many of us are unaware of where it comes from and how it is grown and processed before it even reaches us. This disconnect is a symptom of our more fundamental separation from nature itself.

These days our food and everything else we buy is just one click away. Sometimes I catch myself looking at my daughter, wondering what kind of world she will inherit and how she will relate to it. She is four years old and already perceives a cell phone as an integral part of her everyday life experience, merely because her parents give it so much attention. Does she think trees are as important? Or insects? For that reason and others, we spend time with her in the garden observing the bees, planting herbs, or watching a spider. She helps make dinner sometimes and we ask her to take the kitchen scraps to the composter so that she'll recognize some part of the cycle of life. I have high hopes and aspirations for her, but more than anything I would like for her to have respect for Mother Earth and her many gifts.

I would love to snap my fingers and magically find myself on an organic farm, growing my own fruits and vegetables and raising my chickens for eggs, and then snap my fingers again and be back in the city fulfilling my responsibilities here. Perhaps one day finding the best of both worlds will not entail magic and teleportation. In the meantime, I can make micro changes to my city life that I know will help improve the environment. I do the obvious green things, like recycling, buying locally grown and seasonal foods from local farmers' markets, composting, turning off lights in empty rooms, using cloth bags when I shop, and growing an organic herb garden. But the question I ask every day is, "What is one more small thing I can do in order to make a bigger difference?" I've learned that it need not be drastic. Every step, I believe, matters.

I am often asked, "How do I make the switch, it seems so intimidating?" or "Does organic *really* make a difference to my family's health?" and "Does my lifestyle really affect the environment?" You may be asking yourself these very questions right now. This book will provide some answers to those questions and at the very least, help you take a step in the right direction.

Going green and organic is easier than you think; it's about taking small steps that are manageable for you and fit into your everyday life. And, undoubtedly, green and organic habits go hand-in-hand; you really can't have one without the other. If one is making the conscious choice to eat organic food, one is making a green choice. If you choose to drive a greener car, you will probably find it rather difficult to drive that hybrid while continuing to eat foods that are laden with chemicals and strain natural resources.

"Green," "organic," and "sustainable" are now part of our everyday lexicon, and it's only a matter of time before they describe the way we all live. Being green is not just for hippies and New Agers, and going organic is no longer only for the privileged. Before the invention of refrigerated freight cars and cargo holds, everyone ate organic locally grown food. Let's do our best to get back to that way of life.

The kitchen is a great place to start. It is the hub of our homes, where the action takes place. It is where most products enter our homes, and where the largest amounts of waste leave them. Let the kitchen be the springboard for this green and organic path we will be following in this book, one step at a time.

what is sustainable farming?

Sustainable farming is essential to preserving our natural resources for future generations. It involves using environmentally sound practices while trying to ensure the economic viability of farmers and their workers. As the U.S. Department of Agriculture notes, the term addresses economic, philosophical, political, and social issues that have emerged in light of the harmful practices of conventional, large-scale farming during the last fifty years. Because the term reflects a philosophy rather than a set of rigid requirements, the term itself is mired in controversy. There are myriad views on what specific practices should and should not be part of a sustainable farming system.

On a basic level, sustainable farmers are concerned with maintaining soil productivity and water quality by avoiding the use of pesticides and fertilizers while maintaining high yields for crops; maintaining a healthy and humane life for animals without the use of antibiotics and hormones; and providing a safe environment and economically viable life for themselves and their workers.

As of this writing, a majority of sustainable farms are small, family-run operations. Supporting them is crucial. It's the best way to discourage the unecological practices of factory farms, which have taken over so much of our food production. Through our purchasing power, we send a message to the retailer and farmer that sustainability is important to us.

here are some good reasons to go green:

1. Supporting companies that have socially and environmentally responsible business practices changes the status quo.

2. Purchasing products made with fewer chemicals is not only better for your health and that of your family, it is also better for the environment.

3. Producing less waste in your household helps reduce the amount going into our landfills each year.

4. Consuming less plastic, paper, and energy helps conserve our nonrenewable resources, like coal, trees, oil, gas, and water.

5. Making conscious decisions when you are shopping, such as buying fair trade, sustainable, and environmentally friendly products, supports indigenous communities and small businesses, and respects the environment.

6. Being a friend to the environment feels really good.

> "A sustainable agriculture is one that depletes neither the people nor the land." —*Wendell Berry*

here are some good reasons to go organic:

1. Buying organic food supports organic farmers.

2. Organic farming practices reduce the level of pesticides and fertilizers in the soil, thereby improving the overall health of the soil, air, and water, as well as our own health.

3. Organic produce has 30 percent higher levels of antioxidants than its conventional counterparts. That means higher antioxidant intakes for people who consume organic fruits and vegetables.

4. Studies have found that organic dairy products, fruits, vegetables, and meats actually taste better than conventional varieties.

5. Farmers who grow certified organic food are prohibited from using genetically modified seeds.

6. Organic meats and dairy are produced without the use of antibiotics and growth hormones.

7. Supporting local organic farmers assists in cutting down on energy consumption. Overall energy use on conventional farms is much greater because of their reliance on nitrogen fertilizers and pesticides.

> "For the first time in the history of the world, every human being is now subjected to contact with dangerous chemicals, from the moment of conception until death." —*Rachel Carson*, Silent Spring

getting out of the vicious cycle

I decided that for me and my family one of the best reasons to go organic was to reduce, if not eliminate, exposure to pesticides in our food. Once I learned about the potentially unhealthful effects of the thousands of chemicals that are being used on our food and their polluting effects on our soil, water systems, the air we breathe, and the wildlife in our environment, I realized that if we did not choose to eat organic, we would be contributing to a vicious cycle.

In the United States, over 99 percent of farmland is still being farmed with the help of toxic chemicals to fertilize the soil and kill insects and weeds. The only way to break out of this system is to make a change. The truth is, if you are not eating organic, you *are* eating foods that have pesticide residues. You may be wondering why our government is allowing these chemicals, namely organophosphates and carbamates, both of which are classified as carcinogens, to be permitted for human consumption. Don't they have our backs? The Environmental Protection Agency, the agency that regulates pesticides in the United States, is currently in the process of updating safety standards to adhere to the Food Quality Protection Act, a law that requires the protection of infants and children from pesticides. Although there seem to be some changes happening slowly through government standards, it is still up to us as consumers to shop for foods that are good for us and for the environment. This is easy to do when you have the necessary information.

did you know. . .

The U.S. Food and Drug Administration estimates that roughly 20 pounds of pesticides per person are used every year. And of those pesticides, at least 59 are classified as carcinogenic.

produce and pesticides

I am often asked which foods have the highest levels of pesticide residue, and it is true that some crops need more spraying than others and some bugs are more resistant than others. Below are lists of fruits and vegetables with the highest levels of known pesticides. These lists are categorized as domestically grown, or grown overseas and imported into the United States. The higher the fruit or vegetable is on the list, the greater the amount of pesticides used, and the greater the health risk. So, for example, among domestically grown fruit, cranberries contain more pesticides than cherries. When shopping for produce, use the lists below to help you choose.

DOMESTIC FRUIT HIGHEST IN PESTICIDES

Cranberries
Nectarines
Peaches
Strawberries
Pears
Apples
Cherries

IMPORTED FRUIT HIGHEST IN PESTICIDES

Grapes
Nectarines
Peaches
Pears
Strawberries
Cherries
Cantaloupes
Apples

DOMESTIC VEGETABLES HIGHEST IN PESTICIDES

Green beans
Bell peppers
Cucumbers
Potatoes
Tomatoes
Peas
Lettuce

IMPORTED VEGETABLES HIGHEST IN PESTICIDES

Bell peppers
Lettuce
Cucumbers
Celery
Tomatoes
Green beans
Broccoli
Peas
Carrots

Source: The Organic Center, State of Science Review, "Simplifying the Pesticide Risk Equation: The Organic Option" (March 2008).

On the flip side, people making this green and organic lifestyle change also ask about the safest conventionally grown foods. There are some fruits and vegetables that require little or no pesticides because they are more resistant to pests or pests are not interested in them. For example, bugs have little interest in eating through layers and layers of onion, and as a result, onions are sprayed very little.

The produce on the list below have a relatively low amount of pesticide residue and are fine to purchase in their conventional form. This list will be especially helpful when you are trying to save a penny, since organic foods can tend to cost a bit more, or if the organic counterparts of the items below are unavailable. To reduce your pesticide exposure further, wash all produce thoroughly before preparing and eating it.

CONVENTIONAL FRUIT AND VEGETABLES LOWEST IN PESTICIDES

Onions	Avocados	Sweet corn (frozen)	Pineapples
Mangoes	Sweet peas (frozen)	Asparagus	Kiwis
Bananas	Cabbage	Broccoli	Eggplant

Source: The Environmental Working Group's Shopper's Guide to Pesticides in Produce (2008).

choosing healthier food

When shopping for animal products such as beef or eggs, it's important to understand the difference between "organic" and "sustainable." The animals raised for organic meat must be given access to the outdoors, which can be simply a door leading to a cement patch. Sustainably raised animals must be allowed to carry on their normal behavior, like grazing and pecking. Organic farming can be done by large corporations, while sustainable farms are small operations. Organic products can be shipped across the country, while sustainably produced products are made and sold locally.

POULTRY, PORK, AND BEEF

The use of antibiotics and growth-promoting hormones is common where poultry, hogs, and cattle are raised, so it's important to shop wisely for meat. Organic meat is the healthiest choice because it is free of these drugs. Some experts believe that humans who ingest these antibiotics risk developing drug-resistant bacteria. Another problem with the antibiotics used for the animals is that they are ending up in our water supply, with unknown consequences.

Organic milk comes from cows that are free of bovine growth hormones (BGH) and antibiotics. The cows have at least limited access to the outdoors, and their feed contains no pesticides. The milk is not necessarily local. Try to buy milk from a local dairy in a glass bottle, even though it may not be organic. Sustainable is the number-one choice. The same reasoning applies when selecting butter and cheese. Buy local when you can.

Milk that is not local, including some organic milk, may be ultra-pasteurized. Pasteurized milk has been heated to 162 degrees F for at least 15 seconds to kill bacteria and prolong its shelf life, while ultra-pasteurized has been heated to 280 degrees F and then immediately cooled, which extends its shelf life for up to two months. How this process affects the nutritional value of the milk is still being studied. Some say it tastes creamier than pasteurized milk.

EGGS

These days egg cartons come with myriad labels, including "free-range," "organic," and "vegetarian-fed." It's not always clear what's behind the labels.

- Organic eggs come from hens that consume feed grown without the use of pesticides, herbicides, or fertilizers. The hens never receive antibiotics and their eggs contain no hormones, although the egg industry claims that no hens, organic or not, are given growth hormones. Compliance with these rules is verified by a third party.
- Cage-free eggs come from hens housed in laying barns rather than individual cages, but this does not guarantee that the hens had access to the outdoors. This term is not regulated by the U.S. Food and Drug Administration (FDA).
- Certified humane eggs are laid by hens raised in barns, without cages. No access to the outdoors is required, but the number of perches and amount of space the hens have is monitored. The certification comes from Humane Farm Animal Care, a nonprofit that works to improve the lives of farm animals. Compliance is verified by a third party.
- Free-range eggs are laid by hens that are raised outdoors or have access to the outdoors. Although the FDA has guidelines about free-range activity, compliance is not verified by a third party.
- "Vegetarian-fed" simply means the laying hens receive vegetarian feed.
- Omega-3 eggs are laid by hens whose feed has been supplemented with omega-3s, which are unsaturated fatty acids that may help to prevent heart disease. The eggs also contain higher levels of vitamin E.

So, given all of these labels, which carton should you grab? The best choice for the hen, the planet, and your health are free-range, organic eggs.

While there is no organic labeling for fish and seafood, there are labels and standards you should look for. Many species of fish and shellfish are threatened because of overfishing, so the first term to look for at the fish market is "sustainable." According to the Monterey Bay Aquarium Seafood Watch Program, sustainable seafood "is from sources, either fished or farmed, that can maintain or increase production into the long-term without jeopardizing the affected ecosystems."

The question of whether to buy farmed or wild isn't simple to answer; it depends on the type of seafood and the location of the farm, among other factors. Environmentally responsible fish farms can produce sustainable fish like catfish and clams while others, located in polluted waters and operated with no environmental consideration or oversight, are more harmful. The Monterey Bay Aquarium publishes a guide with the most sustainable seafood options (see Resources, page 243).

COFFEE

Coffee is one of the most heavily sprayed crops in the world. Coffee growers use pesticides liberally to eradicate pests and diseases. This is why it's particularly important to look for organic coffee. These pesticides end up in the water supply and pollute the soil. While the chemicals do not pass into roasted beans, they may harm the health of local growers and pickers and of the wildlife in the region.

The second important environmental concern related to coffee growing is the destruction of forests to plant coffee trees. According to the World Wildlife Federation, of the fifty countries in the world with the highest deforestation rates (loss of forests) from 1990 to 1995, thirty-seven were coffee producers. Some coffee growers in Costa Rica, Colombia, and other countries are moving toward full-sun plantations instead of the traditional shade-grown production. This requires more pesticides, contributes more to deforestation, and reduces biodiversity. Shade-grown coffee is vital because so many bird and bat species seek shelter in the trees. When the trees are gone, the animals' habitat is destroyed.

The best coffee option is shade-grown, fair-trade, organic coffee. Buying fair-trade coffee ensures that fair prices are paid to the growers and money is given back to the community. Transfair USA certifies more than 500,000 small farmers in Latin America, and licenses importers and roasters in the United States. With coffee prices at a historic low, it's important that these farmers receive a fair price for their crop, so look for the Transfair certified label.

Sustainable coffee has recently become more available. This designation is for farmers who avoid the use of pesticides and fertilizers and participate in responsible environmental practices in the growing and processing of their coffees. This requires a voluntary commitment by the grower and does not involve regulation or certification. The designation of "sustainable" also applies to coffee growers who have always farmed without chemicals but can't afford the certification process for an organic label.

defining "organic"

We've discussed organic produce and animal products. But what does the term "organic" really mean? The National Organic Standards Board (NOSB) created the following definition of organic at its meeting in April 1995.

> "Organic agriculture is an ecological production management system that promotes and enhances biodiversity, biological cycles, and soil biological activity. It is based on minimal use of off-farm inputs and on management practices that restore, maintain, and enhance ecological harmony. 'Organic' is a labeling term that denotes products produced under the authority of the Organic Foods Production Act. The principal guidelines for organic production are to use materials and practices that enhance the ecological balance of natural systems and that integrate the parts of the farming system into an ecological whole. Organic agriculture practices cannot ensure that products are completely free of residues; however, methods are used to minimize pollution from air, soil, and water. Organic food handlers, processors, and retailers adhere to standards that maintain the integrity of organic agricultural products. The primary goal of organic agriculture is to optimize the health and productivity of interdependent communities of soil life, plants, animals, and people."

The above definition gives the consumer the knowledge and understanding necessary to make choices in purchasing organic goods. In 1990 the U.S. Department of Agriculture established the Organic Foods Production Act, whose purpose was to:

1. "Establish national standards governing the marketing of certain agricultural products as organically produced products."
2. "Assure consumers that organically produced products meet a consistent standard."
3. "Facilitate interstate commerce in fresh and processed food that is organically produced."

decoding the label

When I go to the grocery store or farmers' market, I am often confused by the information provided on the labels, especially when it comes to packaged food. The labels on organic food packaging include the following: 100 percent organic, organic or certified organic, made with organic ingredients, contains some organic ingredients, natural, and all-natural. Trying to interpret labels can be frustrating when you are changing your buying habits and want to put the healthiest food available on the table. Although some organizations and organic advocates view the organic labeling system as antiquated, it remains today's standard. What does it all mean?

- If a farm or company wants to label a product "100 percent organic" it must contain 100 percent organically produced ingredients, except for salt or water. The label may show the U.S. Department of Agriculture (USDA) organic seal or the certifying agent's seal.

- If a farm or company wants to label a product "organic," the product must contain at least 95 percent organic ingredients, not counting added salt or water. It may not contain added sulfites, but it may contain up to 5 percent nonorganic ingredients that are not commercially available in an organic form. The label may include the USDA organic seal or the certifying agent's seal. "Certified organic" indicates that the product has been certified by either a private certifying agency or a state government agency that is fully accredited by the USDA.

- If a farm or company wants to label a product "made with organic ingredients," the product must contain at least 70 percent organic ingredients, again not counting added salt and water. The label may show the specific organic ingredients, the percentage of organic ingredients, and the certifying agent, but it cannot include the USDA organic seal.

- If a farm or company wants to claim that a product "contains some organic ingredients," the product may contain less than 70 percent organic ingredients, not counting added salt and water. The label may not include the USDA organic seal or a certifying agent's seal.

- In addition, there are some companies who label products "natural" or "all-natural." Although one or more of the ingredients may not have been treated with pesticides, they may not make any claims of organic ingredients. According to the USDA, a meat or poultry product labeled "natural" should contain "no artificial ingredient or added color" and be "only minimally processed (a process that does not fundamentally alter the raw product)." In addition, the label is supposed to explain what is meant by "natural." All things being equal, I will purchase a natural product over a conventional one because at least I know the company may be attempting to head in the right direction.

making the transition to an organic pantry

I realize that these terms may seem overwhelming. The idea of making a big change in your food-shopping habits may seem daunting as well. Take baby steps: Make it a goal to buy organic produce over a two-week period. Then move on to dairy, and then fish and meat. Use the Resources section at the end of this book to help you find sources for organic and sustainable products. For example, the Sustainable Table's Eat Well Guide is extremely helpful; you just type in your zip code and it lists sustainable food sources located within twenty miles. Here are five easy ways to start making the change:

1. Whenever possible buy fresh, locally grown, and seasonal food from farmers' markets. Through direct contact with the farmer, you can learn how sustainably the food was grown. Not everything you buy locally may be certified organic, but it may contain fewer pesticides than conventionally grown produce from a major grower, or none at all. There are Internet guides that will help you find your local farmers' market.
2. Grow your own garden (see page 40). Having a direct relationship with what you grow shows you what organic truly means, and one bite of fresh-picked lettuce or a tomato warmed by the sun will convince you that organic is the most delicious option!
3. Shop at your local co-op. Co-op markets generally source from local growers, buy and sell products in bulk, and offer great discounts.
4. Become a part of a community garden or create an organic food club. Create a support system that helps empower this lifestyle.
5. Start by picking a few of the foods that have the highest levels of pesticides and commit to only buying them in organic form.

Many people are apprehensive about going organic because organic food is usually more expensive. At the moment that is true, but organic food is actually cheaper to produce. Once a farm has been fully converted to organic, there are fewer costs involved in organic farming. The problem is that the demand for organic food is high, and at this point the supply cannot meet the demand. Farmers are scrambling to make the conversion, and this process does cost money and take time. It takes three years to get organic certification, and during that time, the land must lie fallow.

a few money-saving tips

Until the supply of organic food increases and becomes less expensive, you can try these money-saving tips when shopping for organic food:

1. Many stores carry their own brands, which they sell at a lower price point than name brands. This is called private labeling. No matter where you shop, look for organic private and store brands; they will be less expensive.
2. Buy in season and, once again, buy locally. Local, seasonal produce will always be cheaper than produce that is out of season and flown or trucked in from miles away.
3. Buy in bulk and buy only what you need.
4. Purchase from community farms.
5. Buy larger sizes. Prices per unit drop when you purchase bigger jars, bags, or boxes.
6. Look for items on sale.
7. Compare prices at competing stores before making a purchase.
8. Start your own organic garden, of course.

greening your kitchen

One of the first things I did when I decided to green my kitchen was give it a complete overhaul. That meant opening up my cupboards and taking a good look at what was in them to see exactly what was toxic to my family. I wanted only energy-efficient, green, sustainable, and organic products. I dug through cleaning products, cookware, storage containers, appliances, servingware, and anything else that had to do with my life in the kitchen.

I also embraced a process commonly known as Reduce, Reuse, Recycle, and Restore. I got rid of things, gave a few old things a new life by using them for a different purpose, recycled things, and fixed things. In this chapter I will show you what you need to get rid of, what you can keep, and what you need to bring into your home. I'm not suggesting that you go into your kitchen, throw everything out, and replace it all. This is not about being dogmatic, but rather about making changes you feel comfortable with. Start small and then over time make more changes, like I did. I am still making changes every single day.

Remember, you don't have to do everything described in this chapter all at once. Start with one thing that makes sense, get really comfortable with it, and then move on to your next goal and keep going from there. No one is perfect—we do what we can. The goal, of course, is to create a green, safe, inviting, and inspiring place to cook, where all senses come alive. Let's do it!

reduce

First, let's look at what you need to reduce: In today's consumer society it's all about getting the newest, the latest, and the greatest. We all want the cool toaster oven, cappuccino maker, and bread maker, and all the kitchen gadgets that keep our kitchens both well equipped and up to date. As a cook, I love all those things as well. But is it necessary to trade in an older hand mixer with five settings for the new and shiny hand mixer with ten settings, when the old mixer works perfectly well? Will it really improve the whipped potatoes?

Before you decide to buy a new item for your kitchen, ask yourself, Does it operate well? Is it safe to use? Will it make my life easier? In other words, do you simply want it, or do you really need it? If you decide to purchase it, think about where the item comes from. Does the manufacturer have sustainable and environmental standards of production? I encourage you to go online and find out about the company's manufacturing and environmental standards.

One of the goals of a green lifestyle is reducing the amount of waste that comes into our homes. Whenever we make a purchase, the item comes in packaging, which is usually a petroleum-based packing material, such as Styrofoam or plastic. To reduce this waste, consider purchasing the item secondhand (in good condition), or maybe even trading or borrowing one from a friend. When you decide to replace something, consider giving away the old kitchen tool or appliance or selling it at a modest price: have a garage sale or give things away to charity. These are better options than dumping old things in the trash and thus adding to the landfill.

WATER CONSUMPTION

Water is our most valuable resource on the planet, and unfortunately, it is not very renewable. In a class I took on sustainability, the teacher referred to water as "holy water" and told us to treat it as such. In the kitchen we often use large amounts of water for both cooking and cleaning. Here are some ways we can reduce our water consumption:

1. Collect the water you use to rinse produce and use it to water houseplants or an herb garden.
2. Make sure you fill up your dishwasher completely before running the cycle.
3. If you are shopping for a new dishwasher, make sure it has the Energy Star seal of approval. These appliances have cycle and load adjustments and are more efficient than comparable models.
4. Instead of running water in the sink when you're washing up, consider these options: If you have a two-sided sink, fill one side with the soapy wash water and the other with the rinse water. If you have one sink, fill up a bucket with rinse water.
5. Consider installing an instant water heater in your kitchen so you don't have to run water while waiting for it to heat up.

reuse

Reusing things can be challenging because as a society we are so used to using something once and then throwing it out. Disposable cameras, batteries, food utensils, tablecloths—the list goes on. Instead of throwing something out, consider reusing it.

1. Reuse food scraps, such as vegetable peelings, by composting them (see page 43 for more on composting). Think about it; instead of filling up the garbage bag, the food scraps go back into the earth to help grow more food.
2. Instead of throwing out old nonstick or aluminum cookware, use them for various types of storage in the garage. For example, an old aluminum pot is great for storing holiday decorations or hardware. You can also use a small pot under the sink to store kitchen sponges.
3. Once kitchen towels and cloths get too old and scraggly for cleaning up in the kitchen, bring them out to the garage or cellar. They make great oil rags.
4. Save glass bottles. Peel off the labels, and use the bottles as vases. It's fun to collect a variety of shapes and sizes and use them to decorate an outdoor garden party.
5. Stop buying plastic cooking utensils, colanders, and mixing bowls—heated plastic can leach into food. Save the ones you already have. They can be used as children's sand toys. If you don't have young kids, use these plastic things in the garden, for crafts projects, or another way.
6. Stop using plastic storage containers for food and save them to store office, crafts, and art supplies. Never pour hot food into plastic.
7. Use aluminum cake and pie trays under potted plants as drip trays.
8. Cut plastic bottles in half and use them for starting seeds.

I could go on and on here. The point is that instead of throwing things out or even recycling them, which requires a fair amount of energy, reuse them or give them away so someone else can use them. Of course, you don't want to give your toxic nonstick cookware to someone else to use for cooking. But your friend or coworker might be able to think of a creative way to reuse them. Try to give all the things in your kitchen the longest life possible.

recycle

Over half of the cities in the United States have curbside recycling. Although curbside programs do vary, here are the three most common materials that are recyclable. Find out what your city's or town's program is and really take action in your household. Be sure to rinse all food out of containers before tossing in recycle bins as most recycle programs will not recycle the item if there is food matter on it.

ALUMINUM CANS: Did you know that over 50 percent of aluminum cans are recycled? They are the most common beverage container in the United States, and are the most recycled consumer product.

GLASS BOTTLES: Because of the purity of ingredients in glass, bottles have a quick turn-around in the recycling pipeline. Glass can be recycled indefinitely because there is no loss of purity or quality. The various colors of glass have no effect on its recycling capability. In fact, a typical glass container is made up of 70 percent recycled glass.

PLASTIC: Plastic is almost always petroleum based, meaning it comes from oil, a non-renewable resource. Nowadays so many kitchen items are made from plastic that I actually find it quite hard to go to the grocery store without buying something that is packaged in plastic, for example, yogurt containers, containers for berries, and bags for lettuces and chips. Since it is hard to avoid plastic, it's especially important to recycle it.

One of my goals in my kitchen and household is to minimize my purchase of plastics altogether. I try to be really conscious about my plastic purchases because plastics are so bad for the environment. Producing plastics requires not only oil but a lot of energy. They are not biodegradable, and a lot of energy is used to recycle them. Hopefully there will be more biodegradable options widely available some day; I hear they are in the works.

what the symbols on plastic mean

Most plastic is marked with a number from one to seven called a resin code. The number lets you know what type of resin the plastic object is made from. If the number is inside a little triangle, you know the object is recyclable. Below are the resin codes and some common objects on which each number appears.

It's important to pay attention to these symbols because they can tell you how and where an object can be recycled. PET (1) and HDPE (2) are the most common forms of plastic, so they are the easiest to find recycling locations for.

1 PET (polyethylene terephthalate): soda bottles, oven-ready meal trays, and water bottles

2 HDPE (high-density polyethylene): milk bottles, detergent bottles, and grocery/trash/retail bags

3 PVC (polyvinyl chloride): plastic food wrap, loose-leaf binders, and plastic pipes

4 LDPE (low-density polyethylene): dry cleaning bags, produce bags, and squeezable bottles

5 PP (polypropylene): medicine bottles, aerosol caps, and drinking straws

6 PS (polystyrene): compact disc jackets, Styrofoam peanuts, and plastic tableware

7 Other: reusable water bottles, certain kinds of food containers, and Tupperware

Note: Most recycling programs will not recycle any plastic with food on it. Be sure to rinse food containers before adding them to your recycling bin.

paper or plastic? choose cloth!

Consider minimizing or stopping all plastic bag usage, whether it's buying plastic zip-top bags or taking plastic shopping bags from the grocery store. Plastic is a petroleum-based product that comes from oil, a nonrenewable resource. Many plastic bags are recyclable, but unfortunately most still wind up in landfills and will take hundreds to thousands of years to decompose.

Most paper products, including paper napkins, paper towels, and grocery store bags, are made from trees in virgin forests. Often called old-growth forests, they haven't been previously disturbed by human activity. Many of these forests are in North America. The trees are precious to the environment because they release oxygen into the air and provide a habitat for wildlife. As consumers we can let the paper companies know we want paper made from recycled material. Food for thought: if every household in the United States replaced one roll of virgin tree paper towels with 100 percent recycled paper towels, we could save 1.4 million trees.

At the grocery store, at the mall, or in your home, try these options:

1. Use cloth or canvas bags for grocery shopping. Keep ten to twenty of them in your car to have on hand. There are even ones you can fold up and put in your purse in case you forget them in the car. I take my bags everywhere, even to the shoe store. It may be hard to remember them at first, but eventually you won't want to use anything else. (When you don't have a cloth bag with you in the grocery store, choose recycled paper bags instead of plastic.) Some stores, such as Whole Foods, have eliminated plastic bags completely as a bagging option. Hopefully more will follow suit.

2. If you feel you need to use plastic bags, make sure you reuse what you have. Although it may sound unappetizing, wash storage bags and use them until they are unusable. There is even a special bag dryer you can leave on the counter.

3. To store leftover food, use glassware, recycled plasticware, recycled aluminum foil, parchment paper, or aluminum or stainless-steel containers.

4. For kitchen garbage bags, consider using recycled plastic or biodegradable bags.

5. Buy milk in glass bottles instead of plastic ones. The bottles are returnable, which saves glass and gives you up to a 50 percent refund from the store. If you prefer to keep the bottles, they make great vases.

6. Use recycled paper towels or organic cotton dish towels for kitchen cleanup.

7. Offer organic cloth napkins or recycled paper napkins for meals.

toxic cookware and safe alternatives

While I've included ways to be more green and sustainable in the kitchen through the "four Rs," there are other important ways you can green your kitchen, including the removal of toxic cookware and utensils from your kitchen. Aluminum, Teflon, and all other forms of toxic nonstick cookware have been linked to Alzheimer's disease by some studies. Some coatings contain perfluorooctanoic acid (PFOA), a carcinogenic plastic known to leach when heated. Others are made from polytetrafluoroethylene (PFTE), which emits gases that have been known to kill domesticated birds. Find nonstick alternatives that are not hazardous. GreenPan and Gastrolux (a German company) offer safe nonstick pans. Other safe cookware solutions include the following:

1. Stainless steel
2. Cast iron
3. Glass
4. Unglazed terra-cotta (the glazes can contain lead)
5. Coated ceramic
6. Soapstone
7. Copper

Pots and pans made from these materials are healthier choices because few, if any, toxic chemicals are used in their production.

When it comes to utensils, choose stainless steel, wood certified by the Forest Stewardship Council (FSC), bamboo (a renewable resource), or other nonporous materials. Avoid plastic or silicone utensils, which may leach harmful substances.

Always be sure to use the right size pan or pot for the job. A smaller cooking surface requires less energy to heat; matching the vessel to the correct size burner consumes less energy.

seasoning a cast-iron skillet

Cast-iron skillets are inexpensive, and if you season them periodically, they will develop a surface that is almost nonstick. Seasoning a cast-iron skillet is simple. Preheat the oven to 350 degrees F. Lightly coat the inside of the skillet with cooking oil (canola or vegetable oil is best) and bake the pan for 1 hour. Remove the skillet from the oven with an oven mitt, let cool until you can safely handle it, and dry it with a cloth. You can season the pan as often as you like to reinforce the nonstick surface. Or you can buy a preseasoned pan from Lodge Logic.

green cleaners

I could write pages on this topic. In fact, there are many books that go into great depth on the subject, including *Naturally Clean: The Seventh Generation Guide to Safe and Healthy Non-Toxic Cleaning* by Jeffrey Hollender, which I recommend.

Most chemicals in conventional cleaners include Volatile Organic Compounds (VOCs) as well as carcinogenic chemicals. These are known to cause disease with consistent exposure, and the production of these cleaners contributes to global warming and pollutes our water systems.

Some people complain that the alternative—natural cleaners—don't clean as well. But if you are willing to invest some time, I think you will find brands that really are effective. If natural cleaners are price prohibitive, make your own. Here is a list of simple household ingredients that make great cleaning substitutes for the harsher chemical versions. It is from Dr. Alan Greene's book, *Raising Baby Green*:

BAKING SODA eliminates odors and softens water; it can also be used as a scouring powder in the bathroom. To clean your oven with baking soda, sprinkle it on the oven floor and spray with water until damp. Let sit overnight and scrub clean in the morning.

CASTILE SOAP cuts grease, disinfects, and makes a great all-purpose cleaner. This type of soap is vegetable based, rather than animal based.

CLUB SODA removes stains and polishes. Put it in a spray bottle and start cleaning—it's great on windows!

CORNSTARCH cleans windows and removes carpet stains. It works particularly well on acidic liquids, such as juice, coffee, and wine.

LEMON JUICE bleaches, deodorizes, cuts grease, and removes stains.

OLIVE OIL makes a great furniture polish.

WHITE VINEGAR kills bacteria; cuts grease, odors, and wax buildup; and removes mildew. It also dissolves hard water lime buildup on the inside of teakettles. Add ½ cup of vinegar to a kettle full of water, boil, and then rinse well.

green tip

One of my favorite cleaning solutions for coffee cup and teacup stains is a mixture of lemon juice and coarse kosher salt (other coarse grains will work, as well). To clean four stained cups, make a paste from the juice of 2 lemons and 2 tablespoons of salt. Using your hands, rub the paste into the stain and watch it disappear. Rinse with water.

energy-efficient appliances

When it's time to trade your old appliances for new ones, make sure you buy appliances that have the Energy Star seal of approval. The U.S. Environmental Protection Agency and the U.S. Department of Energy came up with a qualification system for appliances that helps you save energy, thereby saving you money as well. Check the Resources section on page 243 for more information.

microwave ovens

When I moved in with my husband, Greg, one of the first things I did was get the microwave out of the house. My mother is German, and in European households, microwaves used to be considered a real no-no for food preparation. The idea of a microwave always seemed so unnatural to me, especially after I saw the science fiction movie *The Fly* (I date myself here).

There are two camps regarding the safety of microwaves. Microwave oven manufacturers and their supporters claim that they are safe to use, energy efficient, and convenient. Critics believe that microwaves are dangerous and should not be used because they emit electromagnetic waves that alter the molecular structure of food. As a result, the nutrients in the food are altered as well. In my opinion, cooking with a microwave renders the food tasteless, too. So do your health a favor and get rid of the microwave, or, at the very least, minimize its usage.

water filters: good for you and the environment

Stop buying bottled water or using a water delivery service and invest in a water filter for your kitchen instead. Not only will you remove chemicals from your tap water, rendering it completely drinkable, you will also avoid buying countless plastic bottles. (Or you will eliminate countless delivery trips to your home by the local spring water company.) Not to mention the money you will save. When you leave the house, take some of that good filtered water with you in a stainless-steel drinking container.

food storage

Choose glass, stainless-steel, aluminum, and nontoxic recycled plastic containers to store leftovers. Use recycled parchment instead of plastic wrap. At our house we reuse zip-top plastic bags from purchased items, such as tortillas. We use the bags to store cheese, and I also take them with me to the grocery store and use them for produce.

grow your own food

Perhaps the best way to connect to the food you eat is by growing it yourself, as organically as possible. You don't need a farm to have a nice garden that yields a delicious bounty; scale the garden to suit your lifestyle. For many, that might mean one or two mini–kitchen herb gardens.

1. Find a 6-inch flower pot.
2. Fill the pot with organic soil.
3. Plant 3 different organic herbs in the soil.
4. Make sure the pot gets some sun, and water it once in a while.

Ta da—a mini-garden! It sounds way too easy, but that's because it is.

There are so many benefits from having a simple pot of living herbs. Teaching children about the life cycle is one reason. Toddlers and young children can help water and watch the plants grow. As they pick the herbs for their dinner, they are one step closer to understanding the cycle.

OTHER GARDENING OPTIONS

If you have the space and the inclination, use a few pots or a planter box and grow several types of herbs. I always have a few pots on a balcony near the kitchen filled with the herbs I use the most: thyme, sage, oregano, and lots of sweet basil, cilantro, and parsley.

You can easily buy bags of herbs at the market, but there are distinct advantages to having your own little garden. The pleasure and satisfaction of snipping or tearing off fresh herbs is a lot more rewarding than tossing a package into a shopping cart. On a practical level, growing your own herbs means you can snip a few leaves for a recipe and not waste the rest.

If you live in a big city like New York, where sunlight (and a window) may be at a premium, or even nonexistent, you can try one of several indoor planting systems on the market. They come complete with a container for the plants as well as a grow light to create a self-contained, portable, full-spectrum light source. (See Resources, page 243.)

On the other hand, you may have a patch of earth in the suburbs or the country that is big enough for a vegetable garden. Be sure to stay away from chemical fertilizers and pesticides. You may need to alter your perception of what fresh food looks like. Chemical fertilizers and pesticides ensure that fruits and vegetables are free of blemishes and produce the most yield per acre; that's what it's all about. And that's why your local supermarket is filled with stacks of perfectly proportioned, visually appealing fruits and vegetables. They are so pristine, they look as suitable for a lab experiment as for your dinner table.

The problem is that the residue from those chemicals can make its way to your dinner plate and into your very cells. By growing your own food, you eliminate the need for these chemicals. Because you're not taking your garden harvest to market, you only have to control a small yield, making it easier to stay organic. Some of the food you grow might have a blemish or two, and a couple of tomatoes might not be perfectly spherical in shape. But that makes them truly beautiful to me. Like people, it's their blemishes that make them much more interesting.

a garden of sunflower seed sprouts

A really easy and fun thing to do is grow sunflower seed sprouts. Sunflower seeds germinate quickly, so quickly, in fact, that kids can practically watch the changes on a daily basis. And sprouting the seeds couldn't be easier:

Place some recycled sheets of paper (such as newspaper or paper bags) or paper towel on a plate and sprinkle some sunflower seeds (with shells on) on it. Place another sheet of paper on top and moisten the whole thing with water from a spray bottle. Keep the seeds moist but not too wet for the next week or so, and the seeds will germinate and pop open. After one more week, you can plant them.

To plant the seeds, place the germinated seeds just under the surface of the soil in a pot. For example, plant 3 to 4 seeds in a 6-inch pot. (You don't have to be precise about the number or spacing.) Sprinkle some soil on top of the seeds until they're just covered, and lightly water every other day (if you have children, let them do this). Keep the seeds moist but do not overwater and in a short time, you'll see the sprouts freeing themselves from their husks as they push up and out of the dirt, heading for the sun. After they grow a few inches, you can pull the sprouts out of the soil and eat them; they are great in salads. Sometimes I like to leave one or two in the pot to grow into full-fledged sunflowers, harvest the seeds, and start all over again.

composting

Organic food comes from organic soil, and the best organic gardening soil is made up almost entirely of compost. While composting may seem complicated, it's actually a very easy addition to a green lifestyle. Compost is essential to a successful organic garden because it replaces the functions of all chemical fertilizers and sprays and provides the authentic nutrients that additives so poorly mimic. Again, just because the use of chemicals produces food that *looks* good doesn't mean it *tastes* good or is good for you. Composting does both, and it does it in a way that promotes a healthful environment for a worm population in your garden. Worms are Mother Nature's microplows and fertilizers. They till and aerate the soil and lay down essential nutrients as they go, and they do it all day long for free.

Perhaps the best thing about compost is that it, too, is free. It's essentially decomposing plant material so why would you pay for it? (Aside from the fact that most city folks do just that when they buy plastic bags of it for their home gardens.)

Another great thing about compost is how easy it is to produce. You begin the process every time you prepare a meal with fruit or vegetables. Kitchen scraps—the tough ends of the asparagus or the banana peel—are not garbage. Embracing this idea can change your waste consciousness as well as your garden. Read it again: kitchen scraps are *not* garbage. Uncooked kitchen scraps are still food, so don't toss them. They are a banquet loaded with life-sustaining food that the microorganisms in your composter will just love to get a hold of.

Follow these easy steps and you'll be on your way to composting at home:

BUILD OR BUY A COMPOSTER

The composter is just a place to allow the decomposition of plant materials in an optimum way. There are many on the market: tumblers, grates, bins, pods, even glorified garbage cans. Some are made from recycled plastic that would have ended up in a landfill. Research the various types online or at a local garden shop and decide which one suits your needs and space requirements. You can also make a composter with stakes and chicken wire or recycled wooden pallets. You can make a functional composter by binding, screwing, or wiring four wooden pallets together, thus keeping the pallets out of the landfill. (A local grocery, furniture or lumber store, or even large electronics outlet will be happy to get rid of their old wooden pallets.) Our composter is a simple wooden box with slats to allow air to circulate.

CHOOSE A GOOD LOCATION

Use a well-drained, level spot, away from walls or wooden fences. If possible, keep the composter away from trees, as their roots will tend to seek the moisture and nutrients in your compost pile. You'll need to set aside 4 or 5 square feet of space; the more space you have, the easier it will be to access the composter. If you have a lot of space and a large garden, you may want to place three composters side by side and use them in a rotational sequence to optimize the composting stages. But for the purposes of this book, I'm going to focus on the easier, single-bin method.

First, lay down a base layer of branches and twigs, about 6 inches' worth. (You can even use a wooden pallet for the base layer.) This will help air to circulate under the material you will add to the composter. You will fill it gradually with layers of both brown and green material.

The green layer can include:
    Grass cuttings
    Tea leaves (including the bag if it's made of organic recycled material; be sure to
        remove staples)
    Cut/dead flowers
    Weeds (leaves only—no roots or seeds)
    Seaweed, pond clearings (leaves or matter found at the top of a pond), algae

For the brown layer you can use:
    Wood material, prunings, wood chips (shredded if possible)
    Coffee grounds
    Recycled brown paper, cardboard, paper towels (without any food on them)—
        shredded if possible
    Leaves (small quantities)
    Egg shells (rinsed and crushed) and egg cartons
    Sawdust, wood shavings, pine cones
    Hay and straw (small quantities)
    Clothes-dryer lint, pet and human hair

Never add the following to your composter:
    Meat or fish
    Grease or oil
    Cooked food scraps
    Cat litter
    Manure
    Diapers
    Barbecue ash

So what about those kitchen scraps—are they green or brown? They're either, depending on what you're cooking. In the kitchen it is not necessary to separate the green from the brown layers in your compost pail. The contents in your pail will most likely make up a brown layer, so when you dump it into the compost pile, add a green layer, unless you know the pail is filled with greens—scraps of kale, spinach, and romaine lettuce, for example. In that case, you would put a brown layer on top of that in the compost pile. Ultimately, it does not matter; the layers from your kitchen scraps will compost.

What does matter is that all of the scraps going into your pail should be uncooked. Raw food has the living enzymes essential for the decomposing process. Cooked food is dead and will not contribute to the process; in fact, it will hinder it.

You'll need a bin or pail in your kitchen dedicated to collecting the scraps that will end up in your composter. This doesn't have to be a large item; ours is a simple stainless-steel bucket with a lid, which we keep on the kitchen counter within easy reach. That's the whole point—to make composting easy and productive.

Put your uncooked food prep scraps into the bin. When it's full, simply empty the bin into your composter and mix it in. If it's your first time and the composter is empty, you'll need to toss in some grass clippings or prunings to cover your kitchen scraps in order to deter any pests.

If you've never composted before, don't worry; you'll get the hang of it. You're basically throwing stuff in a bin and mixing it with other stuff, rather than tossing it in the garbage can. And it's oh-so-eco because you will add other materials from around the house that you used to consider garbage, such as dryer lint, pet hair, and paper products. And those materials will decompose into feasts for worms and microbes in your garden. Composting does take time, though; it will take between 6 and 12 months for your composter to produce dark brown, nearly black material. Add this material to your topsoil. More than anything else, your composter will connect your kitchen, and therefore your household, to the cycle of life. It actually uses your waste to create more life in your garden, which will ultimately end up back in your kitchen in the form of fresh, organic food.

There are two other significant aspects of organic gardening that I do not cover here: mulching and pest control. For the purposes of this book, I've chosen to focus on composting because it is the most direct extension of cooking and the kitchen. For more information on the benefits of mulching and organic pest control, consult the Internet, find a good book, talk to a local organic gardener, or, my favorite option, ask a friend who already knows everything about it.

key terms

Here are a few keys terms to help you follow the "Did you know" boxes provided by the Organic Center.

The **PESTICIDE RESIDUE DATA** are from the annual reports of the U.S. Department of Agriculture's Pesticide Data Program. For each food, the data presented is for the most recent year for which data is available. (The USDA tests about ten to fifteen fresh foods, plus four to eight processed foods each year.) The data appears each year in an appendix.

The **DIETARY RISK INDEX (DRI)** is a relative measure of pesticide dietary risk from a 100-gram serving of food, and is based on the mean residue level of a given pesticide and its toxicity, as evaluated by the Environmental Regulatory Agency in regulatory risk assessments. (For more on the DRI, see the March 2008 report by the Organic Center, "Simplifying the Pesticide Risk Equation: The Organic Option" at the center's Web site, www.organic-center.org.)

ORAC (OXYGEN RADICAL ABSORBANCE CAPACITY) UNITS are a measure of the total antioxidant capacity of food. The more ORAC units per serving, or per calorie, the greater the food is at combating free radicals that can damage cells, trigger inflammation, and accelerate the aging process. Scientists recommend that adults consume enough servings of brightly colored fruits and vegetables to average 3,500 ORAC units per day. (Source: The Organic Center's State of Science Review on antioxidants.)

vermiculture

Vermiculture, or worm composting, involves using worms to transform kitchen waste into compost. It doesn't take a lot of space and can be done indoors, so even if you live in an apartment, you can still set up a worm composter for your herbs and veggies or indoor potted plants. All you need is a container, a starting layer of moist bedding, and worms. Red worms work the best. For more information, I encourage you to research online or get a copy of the book *Worms Eat My Garbage: How to Set Up and Maintain a Worm Composting System* by Mary Appelhof.

starters

PICKED FRESH
TODAY

WITH LOVE

The starter or appetizer is the prelude to the meal, and I believe it should offer a glimpse of what's to come. If the starter is Asian in theme, like Pan-Fried Sake Shrimp (page 71), you may want to stick with similar flavors for the remainder of the meal. For example, the Glass Noodle Stir-Fry (page 161) could follow the prawns. The starter should not be too filling; otherwise, people will have no room left for the rest of the meal. A starter can also be the centerpiece of a light meal. The Quinoa Croquettes with Cilantro Yogurt Sauce (page 63) are lovely with a nice salad.

Try to keep it simple: I prefer unadulterated flavors in my starters, as you'll see in the Bacon and Sage Leaf–Wrapped Scallops (page 67) and Roasted Tomato and Goat Cheese Toasts (page 55). Fresh, pure ingredients don't need a lot of seasonings or complicated preparations to make them delicious. Because I've spent so much time traveling, these recipes borrow from world cuisines and include Italian, Asian, and old-fashioned American flavors. And starters don't need to be fancy: the Curried Deviled Eggs (page 59), my all-time favorite, are perfect for the holidays or parties and are easy to make for a crowd; all you need are tons of organic, free-range eggs.

german potato pancakes with turmeric pear applesauce and chive crème fraîche

MAKES 12 TO 14 PANCAKES

Potato pancakes are a staple in German cuisine. They are typically served as a side dish with a bowl of applesauce, but I prefer to eat them as a starter. This is a take on my mother's recipe. Because the potatoes are pureed with other ingredients, instead of being grated, the consistency of the pancakes is extremely smooth. For a party you can make smaller pancakes and serve them as passed appetizers with a spoonful of the Turmeric Pear Applesauce and crème fraîche on each one. Go the extra mile and top with sustainably farmed caviar from reliable sources. (Wild sturgeon from the Caspian Sea are endangered because of the high premium placed on beluga caviar internationally.)

potato pancakes

3	large eggs
1	medium yellow or white onion, quartered
4	russet potatoes, peeled and quartered
1	tablespoon soy sauce
2	tablespoons minced fresh flat-leaf parsley
	Salt and pepper to taste
	Olive oil for cooking

chive crème fraîche

¾	cup to 1 cup crème fraîche
1	tablespoon chopped fresh chives
	Turmeric Pear Applesauce (page 54)

1. To make the pancakes, combine the eggs and onion in a blender and puree until smooth. With the blender running, add the potatoes and process until they are pureed. Then add the soy sauce, parsley, and salt and pepper, and process until well blended.

2. Heat a nonstick or cast-iron skillet on medium heat and add enough olive oil to coat the bottom of the pan. Pour about ¼ cup of the potato batter into the skillet, making two small pancakes about 4 inches in diameter. Cook for 2 to 3 minutes on one side, and lift up the edges to see if each one has browned. Flip the pancakes over and cook for an additional 2 minutes. Continue making pancakes in batches.

3. Meanwhile, make the crème fraîche. Simply stir the crème fraîche and chives together in a small bowl and refrigerate.

4. Serve the pancakes hot, with the pear applesauce and chilled crème fraîche.

turmeric pear applesauce

MAKES ABOUT 2 CUPS

1. Place the pears, apples, ginger, turmeric, lemon juice, and 2 cups water in a medium pot and cook over low heat, stirring occasionally, until the water has been absorbed and the apples and pears have softened, about 45 minutes.

2. Transfer the fruit to a large mixing bowl and let cool. Run through a food mill or transfer to a food processor and pulse to desired consistency. In my opinion it looks nice when it is a bit chunky.

2	Bosc pears, peeled and cut into ½-inch cubes
2	Fuji apples, peeled and cut into ½-inch cubes
One 1-inch piece ginger, peeled and grated	
2	teaspoons turmeric
	Juice of ½ lemon

COOK'S NOTE: *Turmeric* (Curcuma longa), *a spice indigenous to Southeast Asia, has a bright yellow color and an earthy, but slightly bitter taste. It has played an important role in Indian cosmetics, traditional medicinal remedies, and cooking for more than 4,000 years. It is turmeric that gives curries their beautiful golden hue. Turmeric has been said to ease joint pain as well as many other ailments. I often sprinkle it in my tea for an immunity boost.*

green tip

After you have used up any nonorganic spices, keep the glass jars. Then start purchasing organic spices in bulk to refill those jars. See Starwest Botanicals, in the Resources list (page 243), to order organic bulk spices.

anna getty's easy green organic

roasted tomato and goat cheese toasts

MAKES 18 TOASTS

I love the tartness of the roasted tomatoes with the creaminess of the soft goat cheese in this easy starter. Use multicolored cherry tomatoes to add a little flair to the dish. I served these toasts at my daughter's third birthday party, and they were a hit with both the children and the adults. Feel free to roast the tomatoes a day ahead and store them in a sealed container in the refrigerator. Just be sure to remove the tomato mixture from the refrigerator at least 30 minutes before spreading it on the toasts, as the olive oil may harden when chilled.

1	pint cherry tomatoes, quartered
	Salt and pepper to taste
1	tablespoon olive oil, plus ¼ cup
1	baguette, cut into eighteen ¼-inch-thick slices
¼	cup soft goat cheese at room temperature
9	small fresh basil leaves

1. Preheat the oven to 400 degrees F.

2. Put the tomatoes in a small ovenproof baking dish and season with salt and pepper. Add 1 tablespoon of the olive oil and stir. Roast for 1 hour, stirring once more after about 30 minutes. Remove from the oven and let cool.

3. Lower the heat to 375 degrees F.

4. Place the bread slices in a single layer on a baking sheet. Using a pastry brush, coat the bread with the remaining ¼ cup of olive oil and season with salt and pepper.

5. Toast the bread for 10 minutes. When the bread and tomatoes have cooled, spread each baguette slice with a small spoonful of goat cheese and top with a small mound of roasted tomatoes.

6. Arrange the toasts on a serving platter and top every other toast with a basil leaf. You can also cut the basil into very thin ribbons and sprinkle it over the toasts.

did you know. . .

In Italy, Coldiretti (the national federation of Italian farmers) recently declared Sunday the national day of organic and natural products. Italy opens up hundreds of *piazzi* (squares) on Sundays throughout the country, giving organic farmers the opportunity to sell their products directly to the people. I, for one, would love to see the United States dedicate one day each week to organic food.

real deal bruschetta

MAKES 18 BRUSCHETTA

Here in the United States, a bruschetta is normally made with garlic, tomatoes, basil, and olive oil, but in Italy it is often made with fresh mozzarella cheese (preferably buffalo mozzarella). That's what makes this recipe the real deal. Watch as these disappear off the plate. (And to pronounce it as they do in Italy, say "broo-SKET-a.")

1	baguette, cut into eighteen ¼-inch slices
¼	cup olive oil
	Salt and pepper to taste

topping

4	plum tomatoes, freshly chopped into ¼-inch cubes (about 3 cups)
7	ounces fresh mozzarella cheese, chopped into ¼-inch cubes
4	fresh basil leaves, cut into thin ribbons (about 1 tablespoon)
1	garlic clove, minced
1	tablespoon good-quality olive oil
	Salt and pepper to taste

1. Preheat the oven to 375 degrees F.

2. Arrange the baguette slices on a large baking sheet in a single layer. Using a pastry brush, lightly coat each piece of bread with olive oil. Salt and pepper each slice and then bake for 10 minutes, or until golden. Remove from the oven and let cool.

3. To make the topping, combine the tomatoes, mozzarella, basil, garlic, olive oil, and salt and pepper in a medium bowl and mix well.

4. Top each piece of bread with about 2 teaspoons of the tomato basil topping and serve.

COOK'S NOTE: *Save any leftover baguette heels to make bread crumbs.*

curried deviled eggs

SERVES 6

I just love deviled eggs. I could eat ten in one sitting and probably have room for more. I added a little bit of curry to the recipe, giving this classic party dish an Eastern Indian twist. I find that the best place to purchase eggs is at the farmers' market because you can ask the vendors questions about the way the hens are treated and what they are fed.

6	large eggs
2	tablespoons plus 2 teaspoons mayonnaise
1	teaspoon Dijon mustard
1½	teaspoons curry powder
	Salt to taste
	Paprika for garnish
	Chopped fresh chives for garnish
	Freshly cracked black pepper for garnish

1. Put the eggs in a medium pot and add enough water to cover. Bring the water to a boil over high heat and cook for 13 minutes. Drain the eggs and rinse with cold water.

2. Peel the eggs and cut them in half. Gently remove the yolks and put them in a medium bowl.

3. Mash the egg yolks and add the mayonnaise, mustard, and curry powder. Mix well and season with salt.

4. Fill a reusable pastry bag with the yolk mixture and use it to fill the egg white halves. (Alternatively, use a small spoon.)

5. Garnish each egg half with a sprinkling of paprika, chopped chive flowers, and freshly cracked pepper.

COOK'S NOTE: *You don't have to refrigerate eggs if you use them within a week or two. Because we use them so often, we keep a lovely basket of brown eggs on our kitchen counter, creating more space for items that need refrigeration.*

pan-fried tofu squares with sweet chile sauce

MAKES 36 SQUARES

Growing up with a hippie mom in San Francisco in the 1970s was always an adventure. I remember trips to co-op health food stores with large bins of nutritional yeast flakes. You can still find them in most health food stores (check the supplement aisle or look online). Yeast flakes are a great source of protein and are high in B vitamins. Although they are considered a supplement, they can be used for cooking. Here they make a nice breading for the tofu.

½	cup olive oil, plus 1 tablespoon
1	scant cup yeast flakes
1	teaspoon garlic powder
	Salt and pepper to taste
14	ounces extra-firm tofu, drained, patted dry, and cut into 1-inch cubes
2	tablespoons tamari or soy sauce

sweet chile sauce

¼	cup agave nectar
1	teaspoon red pepper flakes
2	tablespoons minced scallions (white and green parts)

1. Preheat the oven to 375 degrees F. Spray or coat a baking sheet with oil.

2. Pour ½ cup of the olive oil into a medium bowl. In another medium bowl, mix together the yeast flakes, garlic powder, and salt and pepper.

3. Dip the tofu cubes, a few at a time, into the olive oil to coat. Then dip the tofu cubes into the yeast flake mixture. Make sure the tofu cubes are completely coated. Place the coated cubes on a plate or small tray.

4. Heat the remaining 1 tablespoon of olive oil in a large sauté pan. Add the tofu cubes and cook until they are lightly browned and crisp, stirring occasionally and gently. Add the tamari. Continue cooking until the tamari has evaporated and then transfer the tofu to the baking sheet.

5. Bake the tofu for 10 minutes. Remove from the oven and let cool.

6. To make the sauce, whisk together the agave nectar, red pepper flakes, scallions, and ⅓ cup of water in a small bowl.

7. Transfer the tofu to a plate and serve with toothpicks or small skewers and the dipping sauce.

soybeans: non-gmo vs. gmo

Tofu, miso, and soy sauce are all products traditionally made from soybeans, which are one of the United States' largest crops. Unfortunately, soybeans are now one of the world's most genetically modified crops. In 2007 over half of the world's soybean crop (64 percent) was genetically modified. The U.S. Food and Drug Administration has stated that genetically modified foods are safe to eat. Foods that are produced from genetically modified organisms (GMOs) have had their DNA altered through genetic engineering. Many claim there are benefits from GMO crops, including resistance to pests, drought tolerance, and an increase in the world food supply. But others (including myself) argue that there are unknown health effects as well as potential environmental hazards in the proliferation of GMO crops.

quinoa croquettes with cilantro yogurt sauce

SERVES 6

Quinoa (pronounced "KEEN-wah") is one of my favorite grains. It's high in protein, low in acid, and has a beautiful nutty flavor. It is an ancient Incan grain, which the Incas believed was a grain from the gods. Look for heirloom varieties with the fair trade symbol. Fair trade ensures that farmers are being fairly compensated for their labor.

Before cooking, make sure to rinse the quinoa thoroughly in a fine-mesh strainer to remove the bitter outer coating. The tartness of the Cilantro Yogurt Sauce, made with Japanese plum vinegar, is the perfect accompaniment to these crispy croquettes. The sauce is so tasty that I increased the recipe a bit so you'll have extra sauce on hand.

1. To make the sauce, combine the cilantro, soy sauce, vinegar, and onion in a blender or food processor and blend until smooth. Stop the motor and add the yogurt and olive oil. Blend until creamy. Transfer the sauce to a container with a lid and refrigerate for at least 1 hour.

2. To make the croquettes, combine the rinsed quinoa with 2 cups of water in a small pot and bring to a boil. Lower the heat, cover, and simmer for 15 minutes, or until the water is completely absorbed. Remove from the heat and transfer to a medium bowl to cool.

3. When cool add the carrot, zucchini, scallion, garlic powder, salt, parsley, egg, and flour. Mix well. Using your hands, form the mixture into patties about ½ inch thick and 2 inches in diameter.

4. Pour just enough oil into a large skillet to cover the bottom of the pan, and heat the oil over medium heat. Working in batches, lay the quinoa cakes in the pan and cook for 3 to 4 minutes. (You can probably cook 5 to 6 patties at once.) When the cakes are golden, turn them over and cook until the second side is golden. (Check by lifting up a side with a spatula.) Add additional oil as needed, and remove any brown bits that accumulate in the pan as you cook.

5. Remove the cakes from the pan and place them on a plate lined with a recycled brown paper bag. Serve hot, drizzled with the Cilantro Yogurt Sauce. Or put the yogurt sauce in a bowl for dipping. Top the cakes with grated carrot and zucchini.

cilantro yogurt sauce

1	large bunch fresh cilantro, stemmed
¼	cup soy sauce
¼	cup ume plum vinegar
1	small white onion, quartered (about ½ cup)
2	cups plain yogurt
⅓	cup olive oil

quinoa croquettes

1	cup quinoa, washed thoroughly
1	medium carrot, peeled and grated on medium holes
1	small zucchini, grated on medium holes
1	scallion, finely chopped (white and green parts)
1	teaspoon garlic powder
1	teaspoon salt
6	sprigs fresh parsley, stemmed and minced
1	large egg
¼	cup all-purpose flour
	Grapeseed oil for cooking

fried polenta with sautéed wild mushrooms and chipotle cream sauce

SERVES 6

A popular dish in Italy, polenta is made from coarsely or finely ground cornmeal. Although it was once thought of as a peasant food, it is now served in fine Italian restaurants all over the world. After it is cooked and cooled, polenta can be cut into attractive shapes and then pan-fried. Here it is cut into rectangular pieces. My mother invented this particular recipe, and it's a winner. The warm spiciness of the chipotle sauce, although not Italian, is a perfect match for the mushroom and polenta duo. Honestly, my family members have been known to lick their plates clean when my mom makes this. (Okay, I do, too.) Thank you, Mom.

1. Bring the water, 1 tablespoon of the butter, and ½ teaspoon salt to a boil in a large saucepan. Gradually whisk in the polenta and cook for 3 to 4 minutes, until the polenta thickens. Turn off the heat and stir in the cheese. Pour the polenta into a greased 9-by-9-inch baking dish. Cover and let stand for about 15 minutes. When the polenta has cooled, cut into 6 rectangular pieces.

2. Meanwhile, cook the mushrooms. Heat a large sauté pan over medium heat. Melt the remaining tablespoon of butter with the tablespoon of oil. Add the mushrooms and salt to taste and cook for 3 to 4 minutes, until wilted. Add additional salt to taste, turn off the heat, and set aside.

3. To make the sauce, put the chipotles, the 1½ teaspoons adobo sauce and cream in a small saucepan over medium-low heat. Simmer until the sauce has been reduced by half, about 15 minutes. Remove from the heat and transfer to blender. Add the tamari, stir, and season with salt. Set aside.

(continued on next page)

---

2 cups water or chicken broth

2 tablespoons unsalted butter

Salt

½ cup quick-cooking polenta

¼ cup finely grated Pecorino or Parmesan cheese

12 ounces mixed mushrooms, such as baby bella and shiitake, stemmed and thinly sliced

1 tablespoon olive oil, plus additional for frying

chipotle cream sauce

1½ chipotle peppers in adobo sauce with 1½ teaspoons of the sauce

1 cup heavy cream

1 teaspoon tamari or soy sauce

Salt to taste

6 fresh basil leaves for garnish

4. Fry the polenta in two batches, about 3 pieces at a time. Heat a large sauté pan over medium-high heat and add just enough oil to barely coat the bottom of the pan. Add the polenta and cook for 2 to 3 minutes on each side, until lightly browned.

5. Divide the polenta among six plates and top each piece with mushrooms. Drizzle with chipotle cream and garnish with basil.

COOK'S NOTE: *If you have more than six people to serve, you can cut the polenta into 16 bite-size squares and top with a much smaller amount of the mushrooms and Chipotle Cream Sauce.*

green tip

Save all those glass jars with lids. They make great food storage containers.

bacon and sage leaf-wrapped scallops

MAKES 8 SCALLOPS

This starter dish has been a hit with virtually everyone who has tried it. Need I mention that the flavor and texture of organic uncured bacon is immense? There is something so perfect about this dish when served at the beginning of a holiday meal; maybe it's the sage. One of your most sustainable choices for the scallops will be wild-caught sea scallops, also known as giant scallops, from the northeastern United States or Canada.

8	large scallops
8	large fresh sage leaves
8	slices uncured bacon

1. Position a rack in the middle of the oven and preheat the broiler.

2. Wrap each scallop with one sage leaf and then one strip of raw bacon. Secure with a toothpick or small skewer.

3. Heat a large sauté pan over medium heat and add the scallops. Sauté for 10 to 12 minutes, turning the scallops with tongs to make sure all sides are browning.

4. Transfer the scallops to a baking sheet and broil for 3 to 4 minutes. Serve hot.

scallop ceviche

SERVES 6 TO 8

When I developed this recipe, there were many arguments among the tasters, otherwise known as my friends, about whether or not it was too spicy. Some people liked the kick and others did not. I like it spicy, but if you want less heat, lay off the chiles: use one chile instead of two. Serve the ceviche with tortilla chips for a play on texture. I recommend using aquacultured bay scallops for this dish as they are grown and harvested sustainably. Bay scallops are in season from October to January. It's also perfectly acceptable to buy frozen scallops and defrost them; the dish will be just as successful.

1. Combine all the ingredients in a nonreactive bowl and stir to mix well. Cover and refrigerate for at least 2 hours, and up to 16.

2. Spoon the ceviche into small (4-ounce) glasses and garnish with cilantro.

COOK'S NOTE: *Just what is a nonreactive bowl anyway? A nonreactive bowl is made from a nonreactive material, such as glaze-free ceramics, glass, stainless steel, or plastic (but we are trying to retire our plastics, right, unless made from recycled plastic). Reactive materials are aluminum and unlined copper, which react to foods with high acid content, like tomatoes. Have you ever wrapped a tomato in aluminum foil and looked at it the next day? The acid burns right through the aluminum, which gives the tomato a metallic taste. (It's best not to try leaving tomatoes in one of your good copper bowls.)*

1	pound bay scallops, quartered
1	cup (about 12 whole) cherry tomatoes, roughly chopped
2	green or red serrano chiles, seeded and minced (about ½ teaspoon)
¾	cup chopped fresh cilantro, plus additional for garnish
1	cup finely diced red onion (½ medium red onion)
1	cup fresh orange juice
⅓	cup fresh lemon juice
⅓	cup fresh lime juice
	Salt to taste
3	tablespoons finely shredded unsweetened coconut flakes

pan-fried sake shrimp

SERVES 6

This is one of my favorite recipes. The flavors of the cooked sake, garlic, soy sauce, and ginger blend together perfectly. It is important to have some crusty country bread to soak up all the juices—your guests will fight each other for the last heel of bread in order to do this.

Shrimp are generally not overfished because they grow quickly and have a short lifespan. The problem with shrimp fishing is that there is a tendency to trawl up other marine wildlife in shrimp nets. So your most sustainable choice will almost always be U.S. farmed shrimp, with the exception of wild-caught Key West and Oregon pink shrimp. Imported shrimp rank very poorly in terms of sustainability.

2	tablespoons vegetable oil
2	teaspoons minced garlic
2	teaspoons minced ginger
1	teaspoon red pepper flakes
12	Key West pink shrimp with tails on, deveined
⅓	cup sake
2	teaspoons soy sauce
2	teaspoons unsalted butter
	Salt and pepper to taste
1	tablespoon chopped fresh flat-leaf parsley
	Crusty bread for serving

1. Heat the oil in a medium pan over medium heat. Add the garlic, ginger, and red pepper flakes and stir for 1 minute. Add the shrimp and cook for 2 to 3 minutes, until the shrimp begin to curl. Add the sake and soy sauce and cook for another 2 to 3 minutes. Add the butter and cook for an additional 2 minutes. Season with salt and pepper. Stir in the parsley and turn off the heat.

2. Serve the shrimp with mini-skewers and bread on the side.

thai fish medallions with cucumber relish

SERVES 6

While living in Paris in my early twenties, I had a Belgian boyfriend. We often visited his father and stepmother in Brussels, and it was there that I learned how to cook these fish cakes. My boyfriend's stepmother, Kathy Zaccai, is half Thai and she is an amazing cook. I loved watching her in the kitchen, and loved eating her food even more. The cool, slightly sweet and refreshing cucumber salad contrasts nicely with the slightly spicy fish cakes. Go for Pacific cod or farmed U.S. tilapia, which are both sustainably harvested white fish. The Thai green curry is widely available in supermarkets and Asian grocery stores.

1. To make the medallions, put the fish in the bowl of a food processor and process until the fish turns into a paste, 45 to 60 seconds. Transfer the fish to a medium bowl. Add the egg, soy sauce, sugar, green curry, scallions, chiles, cilantro and flour and, using your hands, mix together until blended. Form the fish mixture into cakes 2 inches in diameter and ¾ inch thick.

2. Heat the oil, about ¼ inch, in a large skillet. Sauté the fish cakes for 4 to 5 minutes. Flip them over and cook for an additional 4 to 5 minutes. (Both sides should be golden brown.) Sprinkle each cake with a bit of salt before removing from the pan. Transfer the cakes to a baking sheet lined with a recycled brown paper bag and let cool to room temperature.

3. To make the relish, in a small bowl mix together the cucumber, red onion, chiles, sugar, rice vinegar, and ½ cup water.

4. Serve the cooled fish medallions with the relish on the side.

fish medallions

1	pound cod or tilapia
1	large egg
2	teaspoons soy sauce
3	teaspoons sugar
2	teaspoons Thai green curry paste
3	tablespoons coarsely chopped scallions (white and green parts)
2	green or red serrano chiles, seeds included, minced (about ½ teaspoon)
2	tablespoons chopped fresh cilantro
1	tablespoon all-purpose flour
	Canola oil for cooking
	Salt to taste

cucumber relish

½	cup cucumber, peeled, seeded, and finely chopped
1	tablespoon finely chopped red onion
2	green or red serrano chiles, seeds included, minced (about ½ teaspoon)
2	teaspoons sugar
2	tablespoons rice vinegar

did you know. . .

Thailand is a country whose farm economy has been devastated by its dependence on chemicals. The heavy use of pesticides on agricultural crops has left much of the land unusable, and many farm workers have become sick or even died. But more growers are joining the organic movement, thanks to a community of Buddhist monks called Asok, which means "happiness" in the Thai language. This group of farmers has become the leader in Thailand's organic and sustainable agriculture movement.

soups

When I was a young woman in Paris, I became obsessed one winter with what I called the art of soup making. I had purchased a French food magazine that featured fifty different soups from around the world. And I believed that if I could master all those recipes, which were, of course, written in French, not only would I become a more experienced cook, but I would also be fluent in French. At the end of the winter, I went home a little more confident in the kitchen and much more comfortable with the French language. Whenever I make soup, I think about my time in Paris.

I think soup is the perfect dish for kicking off a meal or serving as a main course with a side salad and piece of toasted, crusty, buttery bread for dipping. This chapter represents a wide range of soups, from simple elegant soups to hearty soups and one-pot meals, such as Curried Split Pea Soup (page 81). The flavors span the globe, from Hearty Miso Soup (page 103) and Spanish gazpacho (page 110) to American turkey chili (page 107) and my favorite childhood soup, German Potato Soup (page 106).

a note about sustainable soups

There are a few options available when choosing a liquid soup base. There is water, of course; water mixed with bouillon cubes or paste to make a liquid; canned or boxed broths; and homemade broth. Think about sustainability when you choose your soup base. (In this context, "sustainable" means using a minimum of energy from start to finish.) This chart lists the choices from most to least sustainable.

Filtered tap water
Filtered tap water with bouillon cubes (only organic)
Homemade vegetable stock (page 113)
Homemade chicken stock (page 112)
Homemade beef stock
Boxed vegetable broth
Boxed meat broth
Canned vegetable broth
Canned meat broth

classic cucumber soup

SERVES 6 TO 8

The summer I learned I would be a cookbook author, my grandmother Gail asked me if I had a cold cucumber soup recipe. I didn't, but I decided I needed to have one in my arsenal of recipes, so here it is, for her.

1. Heat the 1 tablespoon oil in a medium pot over medium heat. Add the shallot and scallions and cook for 2 minutes, or until the shallot is slightly translucent. Add the cucumbers and stir for an additional 2 minutes. Add the stock and remove from the heat. Working in batches, transfer the soup to a blender and puree until smooth.

2. Transfer the soup to a large bowl. Whisk in the milk, yogurt, dill, cumin, mint, chives, and lemon juice. Season with salt and pepper and refrigerate for at least 1½ hours.

3. Serve the soup chilled in individual bowls topped with a drizzle of olive oil and a mint leaf. Add the chopped fresh tomato for color, if desired.

1	tablespoon olive oil, plus additional for drizzling on the soup
1	medium shallot, finely chopped
2	scallions, coarsely chopped (white and green parts)
3	pounds large cucumbers, peeled, seeded, and cut into 1-inch cubes
4	cups Chicken Stock (page 112)
1	cup whole milk
2	cups plain yogurt
2	teaspoons minced fresh dill
1½	teaspoons ground cumin
2	teaspoons minced fresh mint
2	teaspoons minced fresh chives
2	teaspoons fresh lemon juice
	Salt and pepper to taste
	Fresh mint leaves for garnish
2	large fresh tomatoes, roughly chopped, for garnish (optional)

fennel soup

SERVES 6 TO 8

I recently learned that fennel is one of the three main ingredients used in absinthe, an alcoholic beverage popular in France at the beginning of the twentieth century. It was later outlawed in many countries because it was considered too mind-altering. This soup won't get you drunk, but it will definitely alter your taste buds. The sweet anise flavor and the creaminess of the soup will delight your palate.

1½ tablespoons canola oil

1 medium white onion, chopped

2 garlic cloves, coarsely chopped

4 large fennel bulbs, trimmed and coarsely chopped, fronds reserved

4 cups Chicken Stock (page 112)

Salt to taste

2 teaspoons ground toasted fennel seeds (see Cook's Note)

1. Heat the oil in a medium to large pot over medium heat. Add the onion and cook for 4 to 5 minutes, until the onion is translucent. Add the garlic and stir for 1 minute. Add the fennel and stock, bring to a boil, and simmer, uncovered, over low heat for 20 to 30 minutes, until the fennel is fork-tender.

2. Working in batches, transfer the soup to a blender and puree until smooth. Return the soup to the pot, season with salt, and reheat on a low flame. Add the ground fennel seeds and mix well. Ladle into individual bowls. Chop the reserved fennel fronds and sprinkle over the top.

COOK'S NOTE: *To toast the fennel seeds, put them in a small skillet over medium-high heat and stir constantly (so they don't burn) until the seeds begin to release their aroma and brown slightly, 3 to 4 minutes. Transfer to a small bowl and let cool completely. To grind the fennel seeds, pulse them in a small food processor for 5 to 10 seconds. If you don't have a small food processor, grind them with a mortar and pestle or a clean coffee grinder.*

anna getty's easy green organic

curried split pea soup

SERVES 6 TO 8

Split pea soup is a classic. This is a thick, hearty soup that is truly a meal in a bowl. A dash of curry powder and turmeric takes it to another level. Even my four-year-old daughter knows split peas are a healthful choice: they are packed with protein as well as fiber. Unlike for most other dried legumes, it is not necessary to soak peas overnight.

1	tablespoon olive oil
1	medium yellow or white onion, sliced ¼ inch thick
2	teaspoons mustard seeds
5	teaspoons yellow curry powder
1	teaspoon turmeric
1	carrot, peeled and cut into ¼-inch cubes
2	celery ribs, cut into ¼-inch cubes
1	pound split peas, rinsed
2	quarts plus 1 cup Roasted Vegetable Stock (page 113) or water
1	tablespoon soy sauce
	Salt and pepper to taste

1. Heat the olive oil in a medium or large pot over medium heat. Add the onion and stir until translucent, 2 to 3 minutes (lower the heat if it begins to brown). Add the mustard seeds, curry powder, and turmeric and stir well. Add the carrot, celery, and split peas and stir. Add the stock, stir again, and then bring to a boil.

2. Turn the heat to low, partially cover with a lid, and simmer, stirring occasionally, until the peas are tender, about 1 hour.

3. When the peas are cooked, add the soy sauce, season with salt and pepper, and serve.

COOK'S NOTE: *Add water to the soup if it is too thick for your taste.*

winter chestnut apple soup

SERVES 6

This sweet, nutty soup celebrates the cold winter season. Chestnuts are very popular in Europe, where they are featured in side dishes and desserts, but they seem to appear on American tables only at Thanksgiving. Chestnuts are delicious; they have a unique sweet flavor and are lower in fat than most other nuts. They are in season from September through February, but you can find them frozen and jarred year-round. The nice thing about jarred or frozen chestnuts is that you don't have to roast or peel them, which saves you a lot of time and effort. Roasting, though, is your greener option.

1. Melt the butter in a medium to large pot over medium heat. Add the onion, shallot, thyme, celery, and apple. Sauté until the onion and shallot are translucent and soft, 4 to 5 minutes. Add the Marsala and cook until it evaporates. Add the chestnuts and stock, bring to a boil, reduce the heat, and simmer for 20 to 25 minutes. Turn off the heat, add the cream, and stir.

2. Working in batches, pour the soup into a blender or food processor and puree until smooth. Return the soup to the pot and season with salt and pepper. Stir in the chives.

3. Ladle the soup into individual bowls and garnish each with a sprinkling of cardamom and cinnamon, if desired.

(continued on next page)

3	tablespoons unsalted butter
1	medium yellow or white onion, coarsely chopped
1	shallot, coarsely chopped
¼ to ½	teaspoon finely minced fresh thyme
1	celery rib, coarsely chopped
1	Fuji or Jonagold apple, peeled, chopped, and seeded
2	tablespoons Marsala wine
Two	7-ounce jars peeled and roasted chestnuts; or one 1-pound bag frozen chestnuts, thawed; or 1 pound fresh chestnuts, roasted or boiled (see Cook's Note)
4	cups Chicken Stock (page 112)
½	cup heavy cream
	Salt and pepper to taste
2	tablespoons chopped fresh chives
	Ground cardamom for garnish (optional)
	Ground cinnamon for garnish (optional)

COOK'S NOTE: *If you are set on roasting or boiling and peeling the chestnuts yourself, here's how. Be sure to use firm chestnuts, not too soft and not too hard, which may indicate that the nut is rotten. One pound of fresh chestnuts yields about 2 cups of cooked chestnuts, which is what you want for this recipe. Boiled chestnuts are more moist and tender—just the right texture for a soup.* **Before** *you boil or roast them, place a dish towel on a cutting board or countertop. Place a chestnut on the towel. (This will allow the chestnut to "sink" into the dish towel and prevent it from rolling while you cut it.) Using a sharp knife, cut an X into one end of the chestnut to allow the steam to escape. (Otherwise, the chestnut will explode when roasted.) Repeat with the remaining chestnuts. But please be very careful doing this—it is very easy to cut yourself.*

TO ROAST CHESTNUTS: *Preheat the oven to 425 degrees F. Place the chestnuts with the cut facing up on a large baking sheet. Sprinkle the chestnuts with water. Roast for 20 to 30 minutes, or until the chestnuts are tender, golden brown in color, and the shells are beginning to open. Peel the nuts when they are cool enough to handle.*

TO BOIL CHESTNUTS: *Put the chestnuts, in which you have cut Xs, in a medium or large pot and cover with water. Bring to a boil and boil for 20 to 25 minutes, until tender. Drain, allow the chestnuts to cool, and peel.*

green tip

In July 2007, the U.S. Food and Drug Administration issued a warning for Americans to stop eating ginger imported from China. Officials said the ginger contained traces of aldicarb sulfoxide, a pesticide not approved for use on ginger. Side effects from this pesticide include blurred vision, headache, and nausea. When shopping for ginger, look for Hawaiian ginger, and need I say, shop for organic Hawaiian ginger, if possible.

ginger-orange pumpkin soup

SERVES 6 TO 8

Whenever I spend Christmas with my mom, she makes a pot of bright orange pumpkin soup with copious amounts of freshly grated ginger. I've cut back on the ginger to make it more kid friendly, but the flavors still remind me of my mom. She always uses red kuri squash (Japanese pumpkin) for this soup, but you can substitute a Hokkaido or kabocha squash, which also have a beautiful bright orange hue.

1	tablespoon canola oil
1	medium yellow or white onion, diced
2	garlic cloves, roughly chopped
1	medium red kuri squash (Japanese pumpkin), peeled, seeded, and cut into 1-inch cubes
4	cups Roasted Vegetable Stock (page 113)
1	teaspoon ground cardamom
3	teaspoons finely grated orange zest
3	tablespoons fresh orange juice
1	tablespoon fresh lemon juice
2	teaspoons finely grated ginger
	Salt and freshly cracked black pepper to taste
	Pumpkin oil for garnish (see Cook's Note)
	Toasted pumpkin seeds for garnish

1. Heat the oil in a large pot over medium heat. Add the onion and stir for 2 to 3 minutes, or until the onion is translucent. Add the garlic and stir for 1 minute. Add the squash and stock. Bring to a boil, lower the heat, and simmer, covered, for about 25 minutes, until the squash is fork-tender.

2. Transfer the soup to a blender. Working in batches, blend the soup until smooth and creamy. Return all of the pureed soup to the blender and add the cardamom, 2 teaspoons of the orange zest, the orange juice, lemon juice, ginger, and salt and pepper. Blend for another 30 seconds.

3. Ladle the soup into individual bowls and garnish each one with a drizzle of pumpkin oil, a pinch of pumpkin seeds, and a pinch of the remaining 1 teaspoon orange zest.

COOK'S NOTE: *Pumpkin oil, made from pumpkin seeds, is available in health food stores and many grocery stores. You can also find it online. Rapunzel makes a great one.*

creamy butternut squash and macadamia nut soup with roasted poblano chile cream

SERVES 6 TO 8

Many of my friends have tasted this soup, and they always ask if there is cream in it. My response is an unequivocal "no"; it's the macadamia nuts that lend their richness. Unlike dairy, the fat in nuts is a healthful fat. Most nuts are 70 percent fat and 30 percent protein, but by soaking the nuts, you reverse the proportions. The nuts become 70 percent protein and 30 percent fat. Butternut squash, always a favorite during the winter months when it is still at peak flavor, takes center stage in this subtle soup. The Roasted Poblano Chile Cream adds a final touch of New Mexican flavor to this creamy soup. Plan on soaking the macadamia nuts for at least 6 hours. By the way, the Roasted Poblano Chile Cream is also great on the Creamy Corn Chowder (page 109).

1	tablespoon canola oil
1	cup chopped onion (1 medium onion)
2	teaspoons coarsely chopped ginger
1	garlic clove, coarsely chopped
One 2½- to 3-pound butternut squash, cut into ½-inch cubes (about 5 cups)	
¾	cup Fuji apple, cubed (from one small apple)
1	cup macadamia nuts, soaked in water overnight and finely chopped
3	cups Chicken Stock (page 112)
	Salt and white pepper to taste
	Roasted Poblano Chile Cream (facing page)

1. Heat the oil in a medium pot over medium heat. Add the onion, ginger, and garlic. Sauté until the onion is translucent, 2 to 3 minutes, stirring constantly so the mixture does not burn. Add the squash, apple, and macadamia nuts, stir for 1 minute, and then add the stock. Bring to a boil, lower the heat, and simmer, uncovered, for 20 to 25 minutes, or until the squash is fork-tender. Remove the pot from the heat.

2. Working in batches, transfer the soup to a blender and puree until smooth. Serve each bowl of soup with a dollop of Roasted Poblano Chile Cream.

roasted poblano chile cream

MAKES ABOUT ½ CUP

1. Turn the heat on a gas burner to high and place the poblano directly on top of the flame. Allow the skin to char (it will crackle and pop). Continue roasting and rotating the chile until it is completely blackened. If you have electric burners, see the Cook's Note.

2. Put the chile in a bowl and cover it with a plate (or put it in a small pot and cover with a lid). Allow the chile to sweat for about 20 minutes as it cools. Using your hands, gently peel off the skin (it will slip off easily). Cut open the chile, beginning at the tip, remove the seeds, and chop it into small cubes.

3. In a small food processor, combine the chopped chile, the tofu, salt, and 3 tablespoons of water and process until smooth. You may need to stop and scrape down the sides of the work bowl occasionally.

COOK'S NOTE: *If you have an electric oven and stove top, try roasting your chile this way: Set the oven rack as close to the broiler as possible and preheat the broiler to high. Put the chile on a sheet pan and place it in the oven, leaving the oven door slightly ajar. Broil for 5 to 10 minutes, turning every few minutes, until the skin is charred and blistered. (Don't leave it unattended; there's a very small chance it could catch on fire.)*

1   large poblano chile

3½ ounces soft silken tofu

⅓   teaspoon salt

roasted red pepper and tomato soup with garlic and parmesan croutons

SERVES 6 TO 8

As a busy mom, I usually buy boxed roasted red pepper and tomato soup as a timesaver. There is nothing wrong with a good-quality organic boxed soup, I say. Bottom line, boxed soups are convenient, processed with fewer preservatives than canned, and the good ones actually taste delicious. Ask my daughter! I decided to create a version that is just as tasty as our beloved boxed version and is relatively quick and easy. The croutons add a little bit of grown-up sophistication and a textural crunch, which are just what this velvety soup needs.

2	tablespoons canola oil
1	carrot, peeled and chopped
1	shallot, chopped
1½	cups chopped onion (about 1 large onion)
2	teaspoons garlic powder
Two 14½-ounce cans diced roasted tomatoes with their juice	
One 17-ounce jar roasted red peppers, drained and coarsely chopped	
2	cups Roasted Vegetable Stock (page 113)
¾	cup heavy cream
½	teaspoon salt
½	teaspoon pepper
	Garlic and Parmesan Croutons for garnish (page 90)

1. Heat the oil in a large pot over medium-high heat. Add the carrot, shallot, onion, and garlic powder. Cook for 4 to 5 minutes, until the carrots have softened slightly and the onion is translucent. Add the tomatoes and their juice, roasted red peppers, and stock; bring to a boil, lower the heat, and simmer, uncovered, for 15 minutes. Turn off the heat and stir in the cream.

2. Working in batches, transfer the soup to a blender and puree until smooth. Stir in the salt and pepper.

3. Ladle the soup into individual bowls and garnish with the croutons.

garlic and parmesan croutons

MAKES ABOUT 2 CUPS

1. Heat the oil in a medium sauté pan over medium-low heat. Add the garlic and sauté for 1 minute, stirring constantly. Add the bread cubes and cook, stirring, until golden, 10 to 15 minutes. Remove from the heat and stir in the Parmesan. Season with salt and pepper.

2. The croutons can be made up to 2 weeks in advance. To store, cool completely and keep in an airtight container.

1	tablespoon canola oil
1	garlic clove, minced
2 to 3	heels country bread, lightly toasted and cut into ¼-inch cubes (about 2 cups)
1	tablespoon finely grated Parmesan cheese
	Salt and pepper to taste

COOK'S NOTE: *You don't have to use country bread for the croutons. Use any 2- to 3-day-old bread you have in the pantry. Remember, waste not, want not.*

To make bread crumbs: Thaw frozen bread. Rip into small pieces, 1- to 2-inch cubes, and place in a food processor. Process with a series of 5- to 10-second pulses until you achieve the desired crumb consistency. To remove excess moisture from the crumbs, spread crumbs in a thin layer on a baking sheet and lightly toast in a 300 degrees F oven for 10 minutes.

wild mushroom soup with peas and sweet potatoes

SERVES 6 TO 8

When I was in my early twenties, I worked for a wonderful small catering company called Reel Food Productions. My boss, Darra Crouch, was a true inspiration to me because she was very creative with the food. This soup is a take on a mushroom soup she showed me how to make. You wouldn't think that mushrooms, peas, and sweet potatoes go together but they do; the soup is at once earthy and sweet. Feel free to experiment with different types of mushrooms.

2½ to 3 cups	mixed wild mushrooms, such as shiitake, baby bella, and chanterelles
2	tablespoons unsalted butter
1	shallot, minced
1	medium yellow or white onion, minced
⅓	cup dry sherry
4	cups Chicken Stock (page 112)
1	small sweet potato, peeled and cut into ¼-inch cubes (about ¼ cup)
1	cup fresh or frozen peas (thawed if frozen)
¼	cup heavy cream
	Salt and pepper to taste
2	tablespoons chopped fresh chives for garnish

1. Put the mushrooms in a food processor and pulse until a paste forms, 2 to 3 minutes.

2. Melt the butter in a medium or large pot over medium heat and add the shallot and onion. Sauté until the shallot and onion are translucent, about 4 minutes. Add the sherry and then the mushroom paste and stir for 1 minute. Add the stock and cook for 5 minutes.

3. Add the sweet potato, peas, and cream and simmer for 5 more minutes. Season with salt and pepper.

4. Serve the soup in individual bowls, garnished with the chives.

magic mushrooms

The renowned mycologist Paul Stamets makes an interesting case for mushrooms in his book *Mycelium Running: How Mushrooms Can Help Save the World*. He argues that through mushroom cultivation, permaculture (an agricultural method that mimics the structure found in natural ecologies), ecoforestry (which emphasizes holistic practices that strive to regenerate ecosystems), and bioremediation (the process of bringing fungi to improve a natural environment that has been chemically altered by contaminants and soil enhancement), people could create very special mushroom farms. These farms could, according to Stamets, become "healing arts centers, steering ecological evolution for the benefit of humans living in harmony" with the environment.

That is a lot of responsibility for each little mushroom. Until that happens, we can enjoy these magical fungi in our kitchen. Mushrooms are the fleshy, spore-bearing bodies of fungi, produced in soil or a food source above ground, except for truffles, which grow beneath the surface of the soil. No one can accurately say how many types of mushrooms exist, but in North America alone there are more than 10,000 species, and about 25 percent of those are edible. Mushrooms are often described as "vegetable meat" because of their rich flavor.

Like Paul Stamets, I view mushrooms as gifts from the gods. Their strange colors, awkward shapes, and diverse flavors always add adventure to a dish. Whether dried or fresh, mushrooms bring an unparalleled earthiness to the plate. Considered the plant par excellence for gathering, mushrooms truly are hidden treasures. But unless you have a reliable book or an expert guide, "forage" only in farmers' markets and grocery stores.

While most mushroom varieties are available year-round, take advantage of the seasonal varieties, such as spring morels and fall chanterelles, when planning a dish or a menu. When selecting mushrooms, look for those with firm, smooth flesh; pass on any bruised or wrinkled specimens. Never wash mushrooms before cooking them, as they'll absorb the water; just wipe them clean with a damp cloth. Store fresh mushrooms in paper bags to let them breathe, preferably in their own drawer in the refrigerator so they don't absorb the odors of other foods. It's best not to slice mushrooms until you're ready to use them because whole mushrooms keep longer than sliced. Fresh mushrooms will last for three days in the refrigerator.

Dried mushrooms are another option. They will keep in an airtight container for up to six months. Dried mushrooms can be reconstituted in any liquid, including water, stock, and wine. In general, both the mushroom caps and stems can be used.

Whether you are using fresh or dried mushrooms, feel free to experiment with various cooking techniques. The flavor of mushrooms explodes when sautéed, roasted, or baked, and some can even be enjoyed raw.

(continued on next page)

Here are some of the most common wild and cultivated mushrooms:

BUTTON: Also known as white mushrooms, these are the most common mushrooms found in the market. This white-to-beige-colored variety is mild in flavor and is available in three sizes: small, medium, and large.

CHANTERELLE: This wild mushroom ranges in color from pale yellow to bright orange and has a nutty flavor. Chanterelles are wonderful served raw in salads and in cooked dishes, such as risottos and soups. Just add them late in the cooking process so they don't toughen up. Chanterelle season runs from September through early December.

CREMINI: These brown mushrooms are a variation of the button mushroom but with a more pronounced flavor. With round caps averaging 1 inch in diameter, they're available fresh year-round. Creminis can be served both raw and cooked.

ENOKI: These white, stringy mushrooms with a mild, sweet flavor originated in Japan. They're usually served raw or lightly cooked and are an excellent source of vitamin D. Before eating, be sure to cut away the clump at the bottom of the mushroom. Enoki can be found fresh year-round, but they're also available canned.

MOREL: This wild mushroom variety is among the most expensive. Light tan to dark brown in color with honeycombed, hollow caps and hollow stems, morels are often compared to truffles. They add a very rich flavor to dishes and are best when simply sautéed in butter. Found fresh in the markets from spring to early summer, they are also available canned and dried.

OYSTER: This fan-shaped mushroom is pale gray to deep tan in color. Oyster mushrooms have a delicate, almost peppery flavor and can be eaten raw, although they're usually cooked. Available fresh year-round, oyster mushrooms are also available canned.

PORCINI: Also known as cèpes, porcini mushrooms have a nutty, buttery flavor and are most readily available dried. When fresh, these large wild mushrooms are deep brown in color and lack the gills found in most mushrooms. Fresh porcini are hard to find, but are available twice a year, in late spring and fall. Soak dried porcini in liquid for at least 20 minutes before using.

PORTOBELLO: These large brown mushrooms are simply larger cremini, with a flat cap about 4 to 6 inches in diameter. The stems are too tough to eat but can be saved to make soups or stocks. This variety has a concentrated meaty flavor and firm texture and is usually grilled or baked.

SHIITAKE: Also known as Chinese black mushrooms, this light tan to dark brown variety of cultivated mushroom has a rich, meaty flavor that makes it ideal for sautéing and baking. The stems are inedible but can be used to flavor stocks and soups. Although available year-round, their true season is spring and fall.

TRUFFLE: The *grande dame* of wild mushrooms, these stemless, knobby fungi are hunted in the fall, predominantly in Italy and France. Both black and white varieties exist; Italy is best known for its white truffles, while France is known for its black ones. Because fresh truffles are so scarce, they are expensive, selling for more than $2,500 per pound. In the United States, Oregon is the leading source of both black and white truffles, which are in season from January through April and are less expensive than their European counterparts. Fresh truffles are grated over mild-flavored fare, such as egg and pasta dishes, which showcase the truffle's earthy flavor. But if fresh truffles are out of your price range, don't despair; there are several truffle products available that will add a truffle flavor, including truffle butter, truffle oil, truffle paste, and truffle salt.

carrot and cashew soup with parsley oil

I always find nuts to be a great addition to a blended soup, which is why I've added cashews to this basic carrot soup. Native to Brazil, cashews have a lower fat content than most nuts and are high in copper, magnesium, tryptophan, and phosphorous. The Parsley Oil gives the soup a Mediterranean flair.

1. In a medium pot, combine the carrots, onions, celery, and garlic and cover with the stock. Bring to a boil, reduce the heat, and simmer, uncovered, for 35 to 40 minutes, or until the carrots are fork-tender. Add the cashews and stir. Simmer for an additional 5 minutes.

2. Meanwhile, make the oil. Combine the parsley, garlic, olive oil, and salt in the bowl of a small food processor and process until smooth.

3. Transfer the soup to a blender and puree until smooth. Season with salt. Add water to thin out if the soup seems too thick.

4. Pour the soup into individual bowls and drizzle with generous amounts of the Parsley Oil.

1	pound (about 6 to 8) carrots, cut into ½-inch rounds
2	medium yellow or white onions, diced
1	celery rib, diced
2	garlic cloves, quartered
4	cups Roasted Vegetable Stock (page 113) or water
½	cup cashews, soaked for 1 to 4 hours to soften
	Salt to taste

parsley oil

1	handful fresh flat-leaf parsley with stems, coarsely chopped (about ½ cup)
1	garlic clove
½	cup olive oil
	Salt to taste

saffron cauliflower soup

SERVES 4 TO 6

I love the rich, burnt sienna color of this soup, which comes from the saffron. The soup is rich in flavor, but has a velvety smooth texture. It's a great starter soup to serve during the winter holidays. If you can't find raw tahini, you can substitute the more common toasted tahini. (You can order raw tahini online; it's a good ingredient to have on hand.)

4	cups Chicken Stock (page 112)
⅛	teaspoon saffron powder or threads
1	tablespoon canola or grapeseed oil
1	medium white onion, coarsely chopped
1	head cauliflower, broken into florets
1	large russet potato, peeled and cut into 1-inch cubes
2	tablespoons raw tahini
	Salt and freshly cracked black pepper to taste
	Chopped fresh chives for garnish

1. Bring the stock to a boil in a medium pot and add the saffron. Turn off the heat and let the broth sit for 10 minutes, allowing the saffron to steep.

2. Heat the oil in a large pot over medium heat and sauté the onion until translucent, 2 to 3 minutes. Add the cauliflower and potato and stir. Add the stock to the cauliflower mixture and simmer, uncovered, stirring occasionally, for about 25 minutes on low heat, until the cauliflower is fork-tender.

3. Transfer the soup to a blender and add the raw tahini. Working in batches, blend the soup until smooth and velvety. Season with salt and pepper. Transfer the soup back to the pot and reheat on low.

4. Serve immediately in soup bowls, garnished with the chives.

tahini and its many delights

When I was a child, my mother did not allow me or my brother to eat any refined sugar (this may not come as any surprise to you, if you know my mom). One of the few sweet treats we were allowed was called halva or halwa, a Middle Eastern confection comparable to fudge, which is often made with honey and tahini.

Tahini is a creamy sesame paste made popular by the Middle Eastern dish hummus, a dip made with garbanzo beans, lemon juice, garlic, and olive oil. Tahini from the Middle East is light beige in color; it is made from hulled and lightly toasted sesame seeds. The East Asian version, which is referred to as sesame paste, is less common. It is black because it is made from unhulled black sesame seeds, and it has a slightly more bitter taste.

Incredibly versatile, tahini can be mixed into dressings, dips, and soups, and spread on bread much like peanut butter. It is a concentrated food source and a nutrient powerhouse. Tahini consists of 20 percent protein, it is rich in calcium, and is one of the best sources of vitamins E (a powerful antioxidant that helps prevent degenerative diseases), F (said to play an important role in the regulation of cholesterol levels), and T (thought to strengthen red blood cells). It also contains high levels of many of the B vitamins and is one of the best sources of methionine, an essential amino acid.

Tahini must be stored in the refrigerator once the jar has been opened, where it will last for almost a year.

green tip

To maximize the shelf life of fresh herbs, treat them like cut flowers: cut off the ends and place them in a glass or jar of water and store them in the refrigerator. Herbs will last up to 10 days when stored this way. To save space in the refrigerator, keep your herb bouquets out on your kitchen counter; they won't last as long but will add a nice touch to your kitchen décor.

hearty miso soup

SERVES 6 TO 8

In Japan, miso soup is often served with breakfast as well as lunch and dinner. It is a clear, nourishing broth that is believed to wake up the nervous system as well as aid digestion. It is usually served in small bowls with tofu and seaweed. Miso paste, once only found in Japanese specialty markets, is widely available in big chain health food stores. It is made of fermented soybeans and comes in many different varieties. I prefer white miso for its mild, almost sweet taste. I wanted this hearty miso soup to be more like a meal, perfect for dinner on a late night or a cold winter evening.

1. Combine the onion, mushrooms, zucchini, carrots, and ginger in a large pot. Add 2 quarts of water and bring to a boil. Lower the heat and simmer uncovered for 10 to 15 minutes, until the vegetables have softened slightly, but are still firm.

2. Remove 1 cup of liquid and transfer to a small bowl and mix in the miso paste, stirring until it forms a smooth liquid. Return the miso liquid to the pot. Add the cilantro and scallions and mix well. Simmer for 1 minute and serve hot.

COOK'S NOTE: *It is best not to boil miso because prolonged cooking at high heat is said to diminish the flavor as well as any health benefits.*

1   small yellow or white onion, thinly sliced lengthwise

3 to 6 ounces medium shiitake mushrooms, stemmed and thinly sliced

2   small zucchini, grated on medium holes

2   medium carrots, peeled and grated on medium holes

One 1-inch piece ginger, peeled and julienned

5   tablespoons miso paste

2   tablespoons coarsely chopped fresh cilantro

2   scallions, chopped (white and green parts)

chunky tuscan bean soup
with swiss chard and pancetta

8 SERVINGS

Bean soup is a staple in Tuscany, Italy. It comes in many variations—basically, whatever you can get in the pot. Making this soup is a great way to use up day-old bread, and feel free to use up any leftover fresh veggies, too. Rich in protein, it is the perfect soup for winter. If you can't find pancetta, feel free to substitute bacon (make sure it's nitrate-free and organic).

1	tablespoon olive oil, plus additional for drizzling on the soup
1	celery rib, cut into ¼-inch cubes
1	small yellow onion, chopped
4	ounces pancetta, finely chopped
3	garlic cloves, minced
6 to 7	cups cooked white cannellini beans (see Cook's Note)
6	cups Chicken Stock (page 112)
1	large bunch Swiss chard
2	slices country bread, cubed
	Salt and pepper to taste
2	tablespoons chopped fresh flat-leaf parsley
	Grated Parmesan cheese for garnish

1. Heat the 1 tablespoon oil in a large pot over medium-high heat. Add the celery and onion and cook until the onion is translucent, about 3 minutes. Add the pancetta and cook for another 2 minutes. Stir in the garlic and beans and then add the stock. Lower the heat to medium and cook at a gentle boil, uncovered, for 20 minutes, stirring occasionally. Stir in the Swiss chard and bread and cook for another 12 to 15 minutes. Season with salt and pepper, and add more stock if the soup is too thick. Stir in the parsley.

2. Serve the soup in individual bowls with a drizzle of olive oil and generous amounts of Parmesan.

COOK'S NOTE: *Call me old-fashioned, but when it comes to white bean soup, I prefer using dried beans that I've soaked and cooked myself. But if you are pressed for time, substitute about three and a half 15-ounce cans of cannellini beans. Be sure to drain and rinse the beans before adding them to the soup pot.*

To cook dried beans for this soup, put 2 cups of dried beans in a medium bowl and cover with 2 or 3 inches of water. Soak them for 12 to 14 hours. Drain and rinse the beans and put them in a medium pot. Add enough water to cover the beans by 2 inches. Bring the beans to a boil, lower the heat, and simmer for about 1 hour, until soft. Set aside the beans in the cooking water until ready to use for the soup. Rinse and drain.

german potato soup

SERVES 6

This is my mother's recipe; I grew up eating this soup. German Potato Soup typically has pork in it, but this is a vegetarian version. For some reason my mother always used bouillon cubes. You are, of course, welcome to use canned or homemade vegetable stock (see page 113) or just water, but I have chosen to follow the recipe exactly the way my mom wrote it. The flavors improve as it sits, so plan to cook it at least one day before serving. To me this soup means comfort, warmth, and coziness. This recipe is from my heart to yours.

3	russet potatoes, peeled and cut into ½-inch cubes
2	carrots, peeled and cut into ½-inch cubes
1	celery rib, diced
½	small yellow or white onion, chopped
2	large vegetable bouillon cubes
2	tablespoons unsalted butter
	Salt and pepper to taste
2	tablespoons chopped fresh flat-leaf parsley for garnish

1. Combine the potatoes, carrots, celery, onion, and bouillon cubes with 4 cups water in a large pot and cook at a gentle boil over medium heat until the potatoes are almost tender, stirring occasionally.

2. Remove 2 cups of soup from the pot, transfer to a medium heat-proof bowl, and mash the potatoes and vegetables with a potato masher. Alternatively, use an immersion blender to puree the vegetables right in the pot.

3. Return the pureed vegetables to the pot with the soup and add the butter. Season with salt and pepper and reheat the soup on low.

4. Serve the soup in individual bowls, garnished with chopped parsley.

did you know. . .

In a 2002 test, the U.S. Department of Agriculture (USDA) found pesticides in 90 percent of the conventional potatoes tested. By far the most common residue found was the post-harvest sprout inhibitor chlorpropham: 87 percent of the samples tested positive at an average level of around 1.5 parts per million. This chemical accounts for the poor representation of conventionally grown domestic potatoes on the USDA's Dietary Risk Index. They are number 74, the fifth highest on the list of vegetables recently tested for residues by the USDA.

super easy black bean and turkey chili

SERVES 6 TO 8

Every Thanksgiving we travel to Illinois, and I always look forward to my brother-in-law Les's easy black bean and turkey chili. It's his pre-Thanksgiving special and is always ready for us when we get off the plane. My husband comes from a large family, and Les makes a huge pot of chili to feed the crowd. It's the perfect meal for a cold Midwestern winter day, especially when topped with large amounts of scallions, cheese, and sour cream. The chili is also a perfect topping for nachos or even scrambled eggs. It gets better after it sits around for a few days but it rarely has the chance to, as it is a real crowd-pleaser. Double the recipe if you need.

2	teaspoons canola oil
½	large yellow or white onion, cut into ¼-inch cubes
2	teaspoons ground coriander
2	teaspoons ground cumin
½	pound ground white turkey meat
One 15-ounce can black beans, drained and rinsed	
One 15-ounce can cannellini beans	
One 14½-ounce can black bean soup	
One 16-ounce jar corn salsa	
	Salt and pepper to taste
	Warmed tortillas for serving

1. Heat the oil in a medium pot over medium heat and add the onion. Sauté the onion, stirring constantly, until translucent, about 2 minutes. Add the coriander and cumin and cook for 1 minute. Add the turkey and cook, using a wooden spoon to break it up and cook until no longer pink. Add the black beans, cannellini beans, black bean soup, corn salsa, and ½ cup of water. Bring to a simmer and continue simmering for 10 minutes. Remove from the heat and season with salt and pepper.

2. Serve with the warmed tortillas and toppings.

toppings

Grated cheese, such as Monterey Jack or a mild cheddar

Sour cream

Chopped scallions

Sliced avocado

creamy corn chowder

SERVES 4 TO 6

My husband tells me this is the best corn chowder he has ever tasted. But then again, he is my husband and thinks everything I make tastes the best—bless him. Unlike most chowders, my version isn't too thick because I use low-fat milk instead of heavy cream. I really enjoy knowing that it is lower in fat, yet has a perfect balance between the creaminess of a soup and the chunkiness of a chowder.

1	tablespoon canola oil
1	medium yellow onion, finely diced
1	celery rib, finely diced
½	red bell pepper, seeded and finely diced
1	russet potato, peeled and finely diced
1	pound frozen white or yellow corn, thawed
3	sprigs fresh thyme, minced, or 1 teaspoon dried
2	bay leaves
4	cups Chicken Stock (page 112)
1	cup low-fat milk
	Salt and freshly cracked pepper to taste
	Chopped scallions (white and green parts) for garnish (optional)
	Roasted Poblano Chile Cream (page 87; optional)

1. Heat the oil in a medium pot over medium heat. Add the onion, celery, bell pepper, and potato and sauté for about 5 minutes, until the vegetables have softened, being careful not to brown them. Add the corn, thyme, bay leaves, and stock. Bring to a boil, lower the heat, and simmer, uncovered, for 20 to 25 minutes, until the potatoes are soft. Add the milk and remove the bay leaves. Remove from the heat.

2. Transfer 2 cups of the soup to a blender or food processor and blend until smooth. Return the pureed soup to the pot and season with the salt and pepper. Reheat the soup on low.

3. Serve immediately in individual bowls. Garnish with chopped scallions or Roasted Poblano Chile Cream, if desired.

green tip

These days almost all corn in the market is genetically modified. Rule of thumb: unless it is labeled organic, the corn has been genetically modified. Look for heirloom varieties, if possible; they are not genetically modified.

"Sex is good, but not as good as fresh, sweet corn." —*Garrison Keillor*

heirloom tomato gazpacho

SERVES 4

One summer when I was in my late twenties, I went to visit my best friend in Barcelona, Spain. The thing I remember most about Spain is the gazpacho. We ate it everywhere, in cafes, restaurants, tapas bars, and even nightclubs. It was served in little glasses, big bowls, and cups, and it was poured from glass pitchers. The accompaniments included garlicky croutons, chopped boiled egg, scallions, and basil. It was even available at the grocery store in cartons, like milk and orange juice. I like gazpacho smooth and chilled, topped with olive oil, cracked black pepper, and a heaping mound of chopped cilantro. In this recipe I call for multicolored heirloom tomatoes, but feel free to use modern red varieties. Although this recipe does contain chile peppers, I assure you it is *not* spicy: it just has a well-rounded flavor.

3	garlic cloves
	Pinch of salt
3	slices (about 3 to 4 ounces) stale good-quality bread, crust removed
2½	pounds multicolored heirloom tomatoes, quartered
½	English cucumber or ¾ common cucumber, peeled, seeded, and quartered
½	green or red serrano chile, seeded
1	red bell pepper, seeded and quartered
2	tablespoons red wine vinegar
½	cup plus 1 tablespoon olive oil, plus additional for serving
	Chopped fresh cilantro for garnish
	Freshly cracked black pepper to taste

1. Using a mortar and pestle, crush the garlic with the salt until a smooth paste forms. Alternatively, put the garlic cloves on a wooden cutting board, thinly slice, and sprinkle with salt. With the heel of your hand against the blunt side of a sharp knife, push the blade into the salted garlic repeatedly until a smooth paste forms. Transfer the paste to a small bowl and set aside.

2. Put the bread and tomatoes into the bowl of a food processor and pulse until chunky. Add the cucumber, chile, and bell pepper and puree until smooth, about 2 minutes.

3. Pour the soup through a food mill and then return it to the food processor. Add the garlic paste, vinegar, and salt to taste and continue processing. While the machine is running, add the olive oil in a slow stream, and process until the soup has a smooth and creamy consistency.

4. Serve the gazpacho in individual bowls topped with chopped cilantro, cracked black pepper, and a drizzle of olive oil.

anna getty's easy green organic

If you want to add a crunchy texture to this soup, go ahead and make a batch of Garlic and Parmesan Croutons (page 90).

There are more than 100 varieties of cucumbers grown around the world, but the English is my favorite. Thin and long, the English cucumber has smaller seeds than common cucumbers. It is sold unwaxed, wrapped in plastic. (Common cucumbers are often waxed to prevent moisture loss.) English cucumbers are available year-round, but their true season is May through September.

chicken stock

MAKES 6 TO 8 CUPS

Organic boxed and canned stocks are great time-savers, but I firmly believe that a homemade stock adds that extra something to a home-made soup. You simply can't beat it, and it's the greener option to its counterpoints.

1. Heat the oil in a large stockpot over medium-high heat. Add the carrots, onions, celery, garlic, and leeks and cook for 5 minutes to release the flavors.

2. Add the chicken, thyme, parsley, bay leaves, and peppercorns and cover with 9 to 10 cups of water. Bring to a boil, skim the foam off the surface, cover, and then reduce to a simmer. Continue simmering for 3 to 4 hours.

3. Allow the stock to cool slightly and skim the fat off the top. Strain the stock through a fine-mesh strainer.

COOK'S NOTES: *I realize there is a large discrepancy between 3 to 4 hours of cooking this stock. You will get a beautifully flavored chicken stock after 3 hours, but if you want it extra rich and flavorful and have the time, cook it for an additional hour.*

Storing and freezing instructions: Allow broth to cool completely and transfer to a freezer-safe container.

2	tablespoons olive oil
3	carrots, cut into 1-inch pieces
3	yellow or white onions, coarsely chopped, including skins
3	celery ribs, including leaves, cut into 1-inch pieces
4	garlic cloves with skins on, smashed
2	leeks, washed and coarsely chopped (white parts only)
4	pounds chicken, including necks and backs, cut into 8 pieces (ask your butcher to do this)
5	sprigs fresh thyme
15	sprigs fresh flat-leaf parsley
3	bay leaves
12	whole peppercorns

roasted vegetable stock

MAKES 6 TO 8 CUPS

Roasting the vegetables before making the stock adds richness and a robust flavor. Although it may take more time, it is well worth it. You will impress your guests when you tell them you went the extra mile.

¼	cup olive oil
2	large yellow onions with skins on
2	carrots
2	celery ribs with leaves
6	garlic cloves with skins on, smashed
2	medium potatoes, cut into 1-inch cubes
2	leeks, washed and cut into 1-inch strips (white parts only)
2	fennel bulbs, fronds reserved, cut into 6 pieces each
4	bay leaves
6	sprigs fresh thyme
15	sprigs fresh flat-leaf parsley
12	whole peppercorns

1. Preheat the oven to 375 degrees F.

2. Pour the oil into a medium roasting pan. Place the pan on the stove and heat over medium heat. Add the onions, carrots, celery, garlic, potatoes, leeks, fennel bulbs, bay leaves, and thyme. Cook, stirring constantly, for 5 minutes.

3. Place the pan in the oven and roast the vegetables, uncovered, for 1½ hours, stirring occasionally.

4. Transfer the roasted vegetables to a large stockpot. Add 1 cup of hot water to the roasting pan and scrape up any bits sticking to the pan with a wooden spoon. Transfer the liquid to the stockpot. Add the parsley, fennel fronds, peppercorns, and 9 cups of water. Cover and bring to a boil. Lower the heat, adjust the lid to leave a small crack, and simmer for 1 hour.

5. Allow the stock to cool slightly and strain through a fine-mesh strainer.

CHAPTER 4

salads

I consider salad an essential food group, and I am constantly creating new combinations. I can't think of a day when I don't make a salad, whether it's a simple garden salad of fresh greens; a mix of my favorite veggies; or a heartier, protein-packed bowlful of sprouts. Most days I fill my large bamboo bowl with mixed greens and an array of fresh herbs and edible flowers I pick from my garden. Then I open my fridge and see what I can add: fresh goat cheese from the farmers' market, Moroccan olives, hearts of palm, radishes, a day-old avocado, milled flax seeds or hemp seeds—anything goes. After I top my salad with toasted pumpkin seeds or pine nuts, it's time to think of a dressing and I never make the same one twice. It's amazing how something so simple can be so delicious.

Getting creative with salads has gotten so much easier. Gone are the days of dreary iceberg lettuce; today the markets are full of interesting varieties. I love going to the farmers' market every Sunday morning and buying fresh organic lettuce, including mizuna, mâche, baby romaine, red leaf, and mixed "spicy" greens. Some of the salads included in this section can be served as side dishes and others I consider complete meals, like the **Multicolored Chopped Salad with Horseradish Citrus Dressing** (page 124). It's time to get fresh with your greens; experiment with different types of lettuce, sprouts, veggies, dressings, and other pantry items and see what healthful, tasty creations you can come up with. Hopefully this chapter will be an inspiring starting point for you.

beet and watercress salad
with walnuts and curry vinaigrette

There is a health food store in Los Angeles called Erewhon that has been around since the 1970s. They used to serve a delicious beet and watercress salad in the deli case, and when they stopped making it I had to create something similar. *Voilà*—here it is.

2 medium beets, tops and tails trimmed

½ small shallot, minced

2 tablespoons Champagne vinegar

½ teaspoon curry powder

1½ teaspoons honey

Salt and pepper to taste

¼ cup olive oil

2 bunches watercress, coarsely chopped

Fresh corn kernels from 1 ear of corn

¾ cup coarsely chopped walnuts

1. Steam the beets in a covered steamer insert set over simmering water until fork-tender, about 30 minutes. Replenish the water in the pot if it cooks off quickly.

2. Combine the shallot, vinegar, curry powder, honey, and salt and pepper in a small jar with a lid. Shake vigorously. Add the oil and shake well until the oil and vinegar are emulsified.

3. When the beets are done, let them cool. Peel the beets with your hands under cold running water (the skins will slip off easily). Yes, your hands may turn pink; rinse them with lemon juice later to remove the color, or just wear gloves while peeling. Cut the peeled beets into ½-inch cubes.

4. Combine the beets, watercress, corn, and walnuts in a large bowl. Add the dressing and toss until well coated. Season with salt.

heirloom tomato salad

SERVES 4 TO 6

While a tomato used to mean one thing—a red, round, rather flavorless fruit—today you can find dozens of beautiful, colorful tomatoes in the market. I love the odd colors, shapes, and sizes of heirloom tomatoes, which are at their peak in the summer months. Play around with what you find at the farmers' market: no two tomato salads will ever look alike. The flavors intensify as the tomatoes macerate in the vinaigrette, making it a perfect picnic salad.

2 teaspoons sherry vinegar

3 tablespoons olive oil

1 teaspoon salt

Pepper to taste

1 teaspoon truffle oil, or ¼ teaspoon truffle salt (optional)

2½ pounds multicolored medium to small heirloom tomatoes, cut into ½-inch wedges

6 to 8 fresh basil leaves, coarsely chopped

1. In a jar with a lid combine the vinegar, olive oil, salt, pepper, and truffle oil (if using). Shake vigorously until well mixed.

2. Put the tomatoes and basil in a medium bowl and add the dressing. If using the truffle salt, sprinkle over the salad and gently mix until well coated. This salad tends to get a little soggy if it sits longer than a day, so be sure to eat it the day you prepare it.

did you know. . .

About half of the tomatoes tested in 2004 contained pesticide residues. The frequency and levels of pesticides in imported tomatoes exceed those in domestic fruit, leading to a value of 142 on the Environmental Regulatory Agency's Dietary Risk Index for imported conventional tomatoes, compared to 68 for domestic tomatoes.

tomatoes

Tomatoes are both nutrient-dense and nutrient-diverse. One medium tomato provides 40 percent of an adult's daily need for vitamin C and 20 percent of the daily requirement for vitamin A. They are also the major source of lycopene in our diet. Cooked tomatoes deliver 511 ORAC units per 120-gram serving, almost 15 percent of an adult's daily needs. (ORACs measure the antioxidant capacity of food.) Lycopene is a proven antioxidant, which has been known to lower the risk of certain illnesses such as heart disease and cancer. It is more readily absorbable in cooked tomatoes. The nutritional benefits of tomatoes come at modest caloric cost—just 25 calories per serving (1 medium tomato).

In 2006, scientists at the U.S. Department of Agriculture reported that organic ketchup has 57 percent higher levels of lycopene compared to five major national brands of conventional ketchup. Their advice to consumers looking for nutrient-dense ketchup brands was simple—the deeper and richer the color, the more densely packed the ketchup is with nutrients, including lycopene.

multicolored chopped salad
with horseradish citrus dressing

SERVES 6 TO 8

This salad has the perfect balance of sweet, salty, tangy, crunchy, and spicy. It was inspired by a salad I ate at an acquaintance's house in Malibu a few years ago. The name of the woman who made it escapes me, but the salad stayed with me.

1. In a large bowl, mix together the lettuce, endive, tomatoes, hearts of palm, pine nuts, onion, mushrooms, radishes, goat cheese, corn, pea shoots, and dates.

2. To make the dressing, whisk together the vinegar, horseradish, garlic, lemon juice, mayonnaise, olive oil, and salt and pepper in a small bowl.

3. Pour the dressing over the salad and toss well before serving.

1	bunch romaine lettuce, cut into ½-inch strips (about 4 cups)
2	heads purple endive, cut into ½-inch strips (about 2 cups)
1½	cups chopped tomatoes
1	cup chopped hearts of palm
½	cup pine nuts
½	cup chopped red onion (about ½ small onion)
3	ounces fresh shiitake mushrooms, stemmed and chopped
½	cup coarsely chopped radishes (about 4 or 5 small radishes)
3½	ounces goat, cheddar, or other semifirm cheese, cut into ½-inch cubes
1	cup fresh corn kernels (about 2 ears corn)
1	cup pea shoots, chopped (optional)
5	dates, coarsely chopped (about ½ cup)

horseradish citrus dressing

1	tablespoon Champagne vinegar
4	teaspoons freshly grated or prepared horseradish
2	teaspoons minced garlic
3	tablespoons fresh lemon juice
2	tablespoons mayonnaise
¼	cup olive oil
	Salt and pepper to taste

summer zucchini salad with pine nuts and parmesan

SERVES 4 TO 6

This is a beautiful, fresh Italian side salad inspired by a wonderful Italian woman named Lalitya. She is a master of the simple and divine. The toasted pine nuts add a nice crunch.

2	large zucchini, grated
½	cup toasted pine nuts
2	tablespoons fresh lemon juice
2	tablespoons olive oil
	Salt and pepper to taste
½	cup coarsely grated Parmesan cheese

1. In a medium bowl, mix together the zucchini and pine nuts.

2. In a jar with a lid, combine the lemon juice, olive oil, and salt and pepper. Shake well until the olive oil and lemon juice have emulsified. Pour the dressing over the zucchini and mix well. Stir in the Parmesan and continue stirring just until just blended; don't overmix.

did you know. . .
That since 1998, Italy has been the European country with the highest number of organic farms and its organic sector is exhibiting one of the largest annual average growth rates in the European Union.

arugula and strawberry salad
with pumpkin seeds and lemon vinaigrette

SERVES 4 TO 6

Although arugula is a peppery lettuce, it's a versatile one. It tastes great grilled or stirred into hot pasta, and it makes a wonderful pizza topping. In this dish the sweetness of the strawberries and the tartness of the dressing balance out the spiciness of the arugula.

1. In a large bowl, combine the arugula, strawberries, and pumpkin seeds.

2. To make the vinaigrette, in a small bowl, whisk together the lemon juice, agave nectar, and olive oil. Season with salt and pepper.

3. Pour the dressing over the arugula and gently toss. Garnish each serving with a pinch of lemon zest and an edible flower.

1   large bunch arugula, chopped (about 5 cups)

6 to 8 fresh strawberries, sliced

½   cup pumpkin seeds

lemon vinaigrette

Juice of 2 lemons (about 6 tablespoons)

2   teaspoons agave nectar

¼   cup olive oil

Salt and pepper to taste

Grated lemon zest for garnish

Edible flowers for garnish (see page 129)

green tip

Clean your salad greens with food-grade hydrogen peroxide. Mix 11 equal parts water to 1 part 35 percent food-grade hydrogen peroxide in a spray bottle. Simply spray greens in a colander and rinse with water. It is also a great nontoxic disinfecting cleaner for your kitchen.

edible flowers

Some flowers can do more than look pretty: edible flowers add a visual and flavorful pop to any dish. Cooks around the world use edible flowers for their medicinal properties as well as their taste and beauty. Scatter these garden gems over salads and soups, stir into beverages for a subtle flavor, or find other ways to get creative with them. Just be sure that the flowers you plan to use are organically grown and have never been treated with pesticides or fertilizers. (And never eat flowers from a florist; most are imported and have been sprayed with toxic pesticides.)

Here are some of my favorite flowers to try:

ALLIUM, which is a bright purple flower in the onion family, includes chive and garlic blossoms.

BORAGE, a cornflower-blue blossom with a cool, cucumber taste.

CALENDULA, also known as pot marigold. This bright yellow flower has a peppery, spicy bite. The color will suffuse a dish, which is why it's often referred to as the poor man's saffron.

CARNATIONS, perfect in salads. Cut petals away from white bitter flower base.

CHRYSANTHEMUM, a slightly bitter flower reminiscent of cauliflower. Remove the bitter flower base and scatter the blanched petals in soups, salads, or stir-fries. Or brew a pot of chrysanthemum tea.

NASTURTIUMS, the most common edible flower. The blossoms have a peppery yet sweet taste. Great in salads with their bright orange hue.

PANSY, a lovely flower for decorating a savory dish or a cake. Pansies have a very mild, sweet flavor, so use them mostly for visual appeal.

PURPLE VIOLET, which has a deeply perfumed flavor and is high in vitamin C. It is often candied and used to decorate cakes and other sweets. Fresh violets are wonderful in salads and beverages. Note that African violets are *not* edible.

ROSES, the sweet flavor of the aromatic rose is perfect in desserts.

SQUASH BLOSSOMS, the flower of pumpkin and zucchini plants, this delicious flower is available in late spring and early summer. Very popular battered and fried in Italy.

red quinoa salad

This colorful salad is packed with protein. Quinoa is an ancient grain cultivated by the Incas, who considered it sacred and called it the mother of all grains. It has a rich, nutty flavor and blends easily with a wide variety of other flavors. You can find both red and white quinoa in health food stores and well-stocked supermarkets. I like the red in this salad for its vibrant color. Make sure you wash the quinoa thoroughly to remove the bitter outer coating.

1	cup red quinoa
1	cup toasted pine nuts
1	cup dried cranberries, coarsely chopped
2	small English cucumbers, peeled, seeded, and cut into ¼-inch pieces
4	ounces feta cheese, cut into ¼-inch cubes
⅔	cup chopped fresh flat-leaf parsley
¼	cup fresh lemon juice
⅓	cup olive oil
	Salt to taste

1. Put the quinoa in a fine-mesh strainer and rinse for 1 minute. Transfer to a small pot and add 2 cups of water. Bring to a boil, lower the heat, and simmer, covered, for 15 minutes, or until the liquid is absorbed. Fluff with a fork. Transfer the quinoa to a large bowl and let cool.

2. When the quinoa is cool, add the pine nuts, cranberries, cucumbers, feta cheese, and parsley and toss to mix well.

3. Put the lemon juice and olive oil in a jar. Close the lid and shake until the oil and lemon juice have emulsified. Season with salt.

4. Pour the dressing over the quinoa and mix until well coated. Refrigerate for at least 1 hour.

green tip

Over the years I have saved many glass jars and their lids for storage, and I love using them to make salad dressings. Using the jars helps save on cleanup time and water usage. Instead of mixing the dressing in a small bowl each time I make a salad, I make a double recipe of the dressing in a jar and save it. Whatever oil I use in the dressing helps preserve it for 7 to 10 days. I might have four or five little jars of dressings in the refrigerator at any given time.

warm potato salad with lentils and capers

I am forever grateful to my grandmother, who gave me my first set of kitchen pots. While she claims to be completely uninterested in cooking, my grandmother amazes me with her refined palate and ease in the kitchen. This is her recipe. It is simply divine.

½ cup green or black lentils

2 pounds golden potatoes, with skin on, quartered

½ cup chopped red onion (about ½ small onion)

¼ cup capers, drained

2 tablespoons minced fresh flat-leaf parsley

½ cup olive oil

1 tablespoon fresh lemon juice

Salt and pepper to taste

1. Bring 1½ cups of water to a boil in a medium pot. Add the lentils and cover with a lid. Simmer for about 40 minutes, until the lentils are soft. Set aside.

2. Put the potatoes in a medium to large pot and cover with lightly salted water. Boil the potatoes until fork-tender, about 35 minutes.

3. Drain the potatoes and put them in a large bowl. Add the lentils, onion, capers, and parsley and mix well. Add the olive oil, lemon juice, and salt and pepper and stir until just mixed. Serve warm.

wild rice and chicken waldorf salad

SERVES 6 TO 8

This is what I call a meaty salad. The rich nuttiness of the wild rice, the poached chicken pieces, walnuts, and mayonnaise make it a hearty one-dish meal. For some reason men really appreciate this salad; it must be all that chicken. It tastes best when chilled.

½ cup wild rice

2 teaspoons peppercorns

1 whole skinless boneless chicken breast

2 tablespoons fresh lemon juice

2 teaspoons Dijon mustard

1 teaspoon honey

¼ cup plus 1 tablespoon mayonnaise

Salt and pepper to taste

1 carrot, peeled and cut into ¼-inch pieces

1 celery rib, cut into ¼-inch pieces

1 cup grapes, preferably purple, quartered

1 small green apple, peeled, cut into ¼-inch cubes and soaked in lemon juice

½ cup coarsely chopped walnuts

Romaine lettuce leaves, coarsely chopped (optional)

1. Bring 1½ cups of water to a boil in a small pot. Add the rice, cover, and simmer for 50 to 55 minutes, until tender. Drain the rice in a fine-mesh sieve and set aside.

2. Pour 7 cups of water into a medium pot and add the peppercorns. Bring to a boil and add the chicken breast. Lower the heat to medium and cook the chicken until cooked through but not rubbery, 20 to 25 minutes. Check for doneness by slicing into the center of the chicken with a knife. Drain the chicken and let cool. Remove any peppercorns that may have stuck to the chicken. Cut the chicken into ½-inch cubes, discarding any fatty bits.

3. Whisk together the lemon juice, mustard, honey, mayonnaise, and salt and pepper in a small bowl.

4. Combine the rice, chicken, carrot, celery, grapes, apple, and walnuts in a medium bowl. Pour the dressing over the salad and mix well. Serve the salad over a bed of romaine lettuce leaves, if desired.

did you know. . .

Grapes are one of the more pesticide-intensive crops on conventional farms. The growers' heavy reliance on pesticides shows up in the number of different types of residues found. Twenty-four percent of 739 grape samples tested in 2004 by the U.S. Department of Agriculture had 3 or more types of residues, and 2.1 percent had 6 or more. Imported, conventionally grown grapes topped the list of fruits with a Dietary Risk Index (DRI) level of 282. This relatively high score reflects residues of several high-risk organophosphate insecticides, which are classified as carcinogens.

white bean and tuna salad with fresh mozzarella, red onion, and balsamic vinaigrette

SERVES 6

I consider this salad a meal. Every summer when I arrive in Italy, it is one of the first things I make. I always use the vine-ripened tomatoes and arugula from my father's organic garden. This salad is just so darn easy to make and tastes so darn delicious. The Italian-inspired flavors make it perfect for alfresco dining on a hot summer day, and it's simultaneously light yet filling.

1	large bunch arugula, coarsely chopped (about 5 cups)
2	plum tomatoes, seeded, and cut lengthwise into ¼-inch strips
7	ounces buffalo mozzarella
¼	red onion, cut into thin strips
One 15-ounce can cannellini beans, rinsed	
8	ounces canned albacore tuna
6	olives (optional)
⅓	cup olive oil
3	tablespoons balsamic vinegar
	Salt and pepper to taste

1. In a large bowl, mix together the arugula, tomatoes, mozzarella, onion, beans, tuna, and olives (if using).

2. Mix together the olive oil, vinegar, and salt and pepper in a jar with a lid. Close the lid and shake well until the oil and vinegar have emulsified.

3. Toss the salad with the vinaigrette until well mixed.

COOK'S NOTE: *In the spring and summer you can find wild arugula at the farmers' market. Unlike the larger varieties, this tiny leaf doesn't need to be cut—just throw it into the salad as is.*

asian chopped salad with grilled shrimp

SERVES 4 TO 6

This is a colorful and light summer salad with a zesty ginger-soy dressing. Ask your fishmonger for the most sustainably harvested shrimp available; there is scientific evidence that wild shrimp are higher in vitamin B_{12} than their farmed counterpart.

1. Put the shrimp in a medium bowl. Add the garlic, vinegar, and oil, and marinate for 30 minutes in the refrigerator.

2. Heat a grill pan over medium-high heat and put the shrimp in the pan. Cook the shrimp, turning constantly, for 5 to 6 minutes, until the edges have curled and turned brown. Remove from the pan and let cool. Cut the shrimp into bite-size pieces and set aside.

3. In a medium salad bowl, combine the lettuce, bell pepper, carrot, cabbage, edamame, scallions, and cilantro. Add the shrimp and dressing and toss until well mixed. Top the salad with the slivered almonds and toasted sesame seeds and season with salt and pepper.

10 to 12 large shrimp, peeled and deveined

1 tablespoon minced garlic

2 tablespoons rice wine vinegar

1 tablespoon canola oil

6 cups loosely packed ½-inch strips of romaine lettuce (1 to 1½ heads)

½ medium red bell pepper, seeded and cut into ¼-inch cubes

1 medium carrot, peeled and grated on medium holes

¼ cup thinly sliced purple cabbage

¼ cup edamame (soybeans), cooked and shelled

2 scallions, sliced at an angle (white and green parts)

2 tablespoons coarsely chopped fresh cilantro

Ginger-Soy Dressing (recipe follows)

¼ cup slivered almonds

1 tablespoon plus 1 teaspoon toasted sesame seeds

Salt and pepper to taste

ginger-soy dressing

MAKES ABOUT ½ CUP

In a medium glass jar with a lid, combine the ginger, shallot, agave nectar, soy sauce, and brown rice vinegar. Close the lid, making sure it's nice and tight (you don't want to splash dressing all over your wall), and shake well. Then add the toasted sesame oil, sesame oil, and salt and pepper and shake until the dressing emulsifies. It will become nice and thick.

2 teaspoons minced ginger

2 teaspoons minced shallot

1 teaspoon agave nectar

2 teaspoons soy sauce

2 tablespoons brown rice vinegar

1 teaspoon toasted sesame oil

2 tablespoons sesame oil

Salt and pepper to taste

cold sesame soba noodle salad

SERVES 6

Every year my cousin Karline Schmidt arrives from Germany and stays with us while she attends an acting workshop. She has a few signature dishes, and this is one of them. This refreshing salad is a great side dish to serve with Barbecue Baked Alaskan Salmon (page 167) or as part of an Asian-inspired buffet. It is also a perfect main dish for vegetarians.

1. Combine the soba noodles, tofu, scallions, cucumber, and cilantro in a medium bowl and toss to combine.

2. Mix the tahini, rice vinegar, toasted sesame oil, sesame oil, and soy sauce in a small bowl with 2 tablespoons water. Mix until creamy and smooth.

3. Pour the dressing over the noodles and toss until well coated. Add the sesame seeds and toss again. Cover the salad and chill for at least 2 hours or overnight before serving.

- 8 ounces soba noodles, cooked according to the package directions
- 3½ ounces extra-firm tofu, cut into ¼-inch cubes
- 2 scallions, chopped (white and green parts)
- ½ cucumber, peeled, seeded, and cut into ¼-inch cubes
- ⅓ cup chopped fresh cilantro
- 2 tablespoons tahini
- 2 tablespoons rice vinegar
- 1 tablespoon toasted sesame oil
- 1 tablespoon sesame oil
- 1 teaspoon soy sauce
- 2 tablespoons toasted sesame seeds

COOK'S NOTE: *I love the flavor of toasted sesame oil, which is dark in color and is available in Asian markets as well as some supermarkets. It is often added at the end of the cooking process as a flavor note. A little goes a long way—it has a very strong taste and aroma. Sesame oil that has not been toasted is much milder in flavor and great for cooking. It can withstand medium to high heat.*

warm asian mushroom salad

SERVES 4

It's hard to believe, but this salad is the first thing I learned how to make after scrambled eggs and my grandmother's easy pasta sauce. I was living in Paris at the tender age of twenty-one and discovered shiitake mushrooms at the farmers' market. The rest of the ingredients I just instinctively threw in. The meatiness of the shiitake mushrooms helps make this salad a meal on its own.

2	tablespoons canola oil
One ½-inch piece ginger,	peeled and minced
2	garlic cloves, minced
4	medium shiitake mushrooms, stemmed and cut into ¼-inch-wide matchsticks
2	tablespoons soy sauce
2	teaspoons toasted sesame oil
6	cups loosely packed mixed baby lettuces
1	medium carrot, peeled and grated
2	tablespoons coarsely chopped fresh cilantro
1	teaspoon black sesame seeds

1. Heat the canola oil in a medium sauté pan over medium heat. Add the ginger and garlic and sauté for about 1 minute, stirring constantly to make sure they don't brown. Add the mushrooms and stir for 10 seconds. Add ¼ cup of water and cook, stirring, until the mushrooms are soft and the water has evaporated, 3 to 4 minutes. Add the soy sauce and the sesame oil and remove from the heat.

2. In a large bowl, combine the lettuces and carrot and add the mushrooms. Toss until the lettuce is coated with the soy sauce and sesame oil. Top the salad with cilantro and black sesame seeds.

thai carrot salad with toasted almonds

SERVES 4 TO 6

In Thailand this salad is usually made with toasted peanuts, but the almonds give a fresh twist to this sweet and spicy dish. It makes a great addition to an Asian-inspired meal, and is oh-so-easy to make.

Mix all of the ingredients together in a medium bowl. Refrigerate for at least 2 hours before serving.

6	medium carrots, peeled and grated on large holes
3	tablespoons sugar
3	garlic cloves, minced
1	tablespoon finely chopped fresh cilantro
½	green or red serrano chile, seeded and minced
3	tablespoons fresh lemon juice
2	teaspoons ume plum vinegar
1	teaspoon soy sauce
½	cup toasted almonds

did you know. . .

Thirty-two percent of the carrots tested by the U.S. Department of Agriculture for pesticide residues in 2006 contained 3 or more pesticides. Imported conventional carrots pose greater risks than domestically grown vegetables, and scored 30 on the Dietary Risk Index scale.

carrot caraway salad

There is something so refreshing about raw carrots. The sweet yet strong taste of the caraway seeds is the perfect match for the crispness of this vibrant root vegetable. Caraway seeds are actually not seeds at all but rather the small fruit of the caraway plant.

1. Combine the carrots and caraway seeds in a medium bowl.

2. In a jar with a lid, combine the lemon juice, agave nectar, vinegar, mustard, salt, and pepper. Shake until well mixed.

3. Pour the dressing over the carrots and mix well. Add the parsley and mix again. Cover and refrigerate for at least 2 hours or overnight.

8   medium carrots, grated on medium holes (about 5 cups)

1¼   teaspoons caraway seeds

Juice of ½ lemon

1   tablespoon plus 2 teaspoons agave nectar

2   teaspoons apple cider vinegar

2   teaspoons Dijon mustard

Pinch of salt

Pinch of pepper

1   tablespoon chopped fresh flat-leaf parsley

agave nectar

Agave nectar, also called agave syrup, is a natural sweetener with a consistency similar to honey. Believe it or not, it's made in Mexico from the same blue agave plant that produces tequila. Although it's sweeter than sugar, what makes agave a must-have in the kitchen is the fact that it's lower on the glycemic index than sugar and most other sweeteners, including molasses, maple syrup, and corn syrup. With a 90 percent fructose content, agave is absorbed much more slowly into the body. That makes it an attractive sweetener for those concerned with high sugar intake.

Agave nectar is available in both light and dark varieties. The dark version, which is unfiltered, contains higher concentrations of the agave plant's minerals. This thick syrup is more pourable than honey and it has no discernible flavor. Agave nectar is wonderful in salad dressings and sauces, is great in tea (it dissolves easily), and is perfect for baking and sweetening almost any dessert. If you would like to use agave nectar in a baking recipe that calls for sugar, substitute $1/2$ cup of agave nectar for 1 cup of sugar; you may have to adjust the liquid ingredients as well. (Check out the book *Baking with Agave Nectar* by Ania Catalano if you want to learn more.)

Agave nectar usually comes in plastic or glass bottles and can be stored on the kitchen counter or in the pantry for at least two years. (I prefer glass bottles, the green choice.) Most organic agave nectar is raw, which is even better as it retains all of the enzymes.

creamy basil dressing

MAKES 2½ TO 3 CUPS

One of my favorite restaurants when I lived in Paris was a vegetarian spot called Il Piccolo Teatro ("the Little Theater" in Italian). They made an incredible creamy basil dressing, and I spent three years trying to get the recipe. While they never gave me the recipe, they sold me the dressing, which I carried home in a large plastic Evian bottle. Years later when I visited Paris, I stopped at the restaurant. When I told them I had moved away, they finally revealed the ingredients, but not the amounts or the method—fair enough. Here is a version of my beloved creamy basil dressing. Use it on salads, over fish or chicken, or in soups. Heck, drink it out of an Evian bottle if you like, as long as the bottle is glass and not plastic.

4½	ounces firm tofu
	Leaves from a small bunch of basil (about 30)
2	tablespoons tamari or soy sauce
2	tablespoons ume plum vinegar
1	cup sunflower oil

Combine the tofu, basil leaves, and 1 cup of water in a blender and blend at high speed until smooth. Stop the blender, add the tamari and ume vinegar, and continue blending. With the blender running, slowly add the sunflower oil in a steady stream and continue running the blender until the dressing emulsifies, 30 seconds to 1 minute.

simple creamy tahini dressing

MAKES ABOUT ½ CUP

One of my favorite salad dressings is a combination of tahini, lemon juice, garlic, salt, and olive oil. It's so simple, but adds so much creamy richness to an otherwise simple salad. In a small bowl, mix together the garlic and salt with a fork until you form a paste. Stir in the tahini until creamy. Stir in the lemon juice and then the olive oil and continue stirring until emulsified.

1	garlic clove, peeled and roughly chopped
1	teaspoon ground salt
2	tablespoons tahini
	Juice of 1 lemon
¼	cup olive oil

main dishes

The main dish (other than a simple plate of pasta) was always a scary notion to me as a novice cook. It meant there was the potential for a lot of ingredients and complicated ways of preparing them. And since I grew up in a vegetarian household where the main dish usually consisted of tofu or tempeh, I never really learned how to cook ingredients like fish or poultry. Only later, as a young prep cook working in a catering kitchen, did I learn how to cook fish, poultry, and meat and it opened my eyes to the many possibilities. Now I like to throw together Coconut Chicken Curry (page 170) or Simple Tomato Sauce and Spaghetti (page 157) for a weeknight supper or surprise dinner guests with an elegant filet mignon with whiskey cream sauce (page 174) or Seared Bay Scallops with Orzo and Sun-Dried Tomato Cream Sauce (page 163).

I believe that main dishes are best when they're simple and uncomplicated (surprise, surprise), whether you're serving tofu, chicken, or pasta. Steamed Halibut with Greek Salad Salsa (page 165) is a testimony to simplicity, allowing the star of the dish—the fish—to shine. It seems silly to seek out organic ingredients and then mask their flavor with bold spices and overly complicated flavors. Enjoy the international variety of these main dishes.

ginger risotto

SERVES 4

The beloved ginger root, that ubiquitous Asian ingredient, is paired with Italian Arborio rice in this super-simple risotto. The most important thing to remember when making a risotto is to never let it rest while on the burner: stir, stir, stir! In Italy a risotto is usually served as a *primo piatto*, after the starter and before the main dish. I've included this recipe with the main courses because I think that risotto can hold its own as an entrée, rather than a starter. And it is a great main course option for vegetarians if you substitute vegetable stock for the chicken stock.

7	cups Chicken Stock (page 112)
1	tablespoon olive oil
1	medium white onion, finely diced (about 1½ cups)
1	tablespoon plus 2 teaspoons grated ginger
1½	cups Arborio rice
1	cup white wine
2	tablespoons unsalted butter
½	cup freshly grated Parmesan cheese
	Salt and freshly cracked pepper to taste

1. Bring the stock to a simmer in a medium pot and keep it at a simmer until the risotto is done.

2. Heat the oil in a large sauté pan over medium heat. Add the onion and 1 tablespoon of the ginger and cook, stirring constantly, for 2 to 3 minutes, until the onion is translucent.

3. Add the rice and stir. Stir in the wine and simmer until the liquid is evaporated. Begin adding stock, one ladleful at a time, stirring constantly until the liquid is absorbed. Continue adding stock until the rice is cooked but still firm and creamy, 30 to 35 minutes.

4. Turn off the heat. Add the butter, the remaining 2 teaspoons of ginger, and the Parmesan. Season with salt and pepper and serve immediately.

did you know. . .

Recently published research shows that some U.S. non-organic rice has 1.4 to 5 times more arsenic traces than rice produced in India, Bangladesh, or Europe. This is a great reason to select organic rice whenever possible.

baked portobello mushrooms with avocado and pesto

SERVES 4

Portobello mushrooms are just cremini mushrooms all grown up. The mature mushrooms have a meaty texture and rich flavor that is often compared to steak. Portobellos often appear on menus as a main course, and they're a great option for vegetarians. In this dish, I love the marriage of textures and flavors that come from the baked portobello, avocado, and basil pesto.

30	medium-size fresh basil leaves
1	large garlic clove
½	cup walnuts
½	cup olive oil
	Salt and pepper to taste
2	ripe avocados (not too soft)
4	large portobello mushrooms, stemmed

1. Preheat the oven to 375 degrees F. Spray a small baking sheet with nonstick cooking spray.

2. Combine the basil leaves, garlic, walnuts, and olive oil in a food processor and process until smooth. Transfer to a small bowl, season with salt and pepper, and mix well.

3. Cut the avocados in half and remove the pits. Slice each avocado half into 8 to 10 slices ⅓ inch thick and then use a spoon or fork to scoop the flesh from the peel.

4. Place the mushrooms on the baking sheet and top with half of the avocado slices, fanning out the slices to cover the mushroom caps. Spoon 2 to 3 tablespoons of pesto on top of the avocado slices on each mushroom. Bake for 30 minutes.

5. Serve while still warm but not too hot.

spicy garbanzo bean burritos with cucumber yogurt sauce

SERVES 6

In this dish the typical Mexican burrito gets a twist with these atypical ingredients. This recipe is inspired by the flavors of Morocco. The garbanzo beans, cumin, and coriander are the usual suspects in North African cuisine. Here they come together with a creamy yogurt sauce for an easy, satisfying meal.

2	tablespoons vegetable oil
1	tablespoon minced garlic
1½	cups thinly sliced onion (about 1 medium onion)
⅔	cup thinly sliced red bell pepper
2	teaspoons ground coriander
1	teaspoon ground cumin
½	teaspoon red pepper flakes
1	teaspoon paprika
Two	15-ounce cans garbanzo beans (chickpeas), drained
	Salt and pepper to taste
2	tablespoons chopped fresh cilantro
6	large flour tortillas

1. Heat a large sauté pan over medium heat and add the oil. Add the garlic, onion, and bell pepper and cook for 6 minutes. Add the coriander, cumin, red pepper flakes, and paprika and mix well. Add the garbanzo beans and cook for 5 minutes, stirring constantly. Season with salt and pepper and then stir in the cilantro.

2. While the garbanzos are cooking, make the sauce. Mix together all of the ingredients in a small bowl.

3. Spoon ½ cup of the garbanzo bean mixture onto each tortilla and top with some yogurt sauce. Roll up the tortillas tightly and serve.

COOK'S NOTE: *Add a slice or two of avocado to give each burrito extra richness.*

cucumber yogurt sauce

½	cup plain yogurt
1	small cucumber, peeled, seeded, and grated on medium holes (about ½ cup)
½	teaspoon paprika
	Salt and pepper to taste

pea tendril and goat cheese frittata

SERVES 6

Pea tendrils are worth their weight in gold. I am such a fanatic about them that I've actually had face-offs with people at the farmers' market when the crate of pea tendrils is almost empty. I now grow my own to avoid these types of encounters. The tendrils are the young leaves and shoots of the snow pea plant, and they have a subtle flavor of sweet peas and spinach. Their delicate flavor comes alive in this simple egg dish, which can be served at breakfast, lunch, or dinner.

10	large eggs
	Salt and pepper to taste
2	ounces soft goat cheese, crumbled
1½	tablespoons unsalted butter
1	cup finely diced shallots (about 4 small shallots)
2	cups chopped purple or green scallions (1 large bunch, white and green parts)
½	cup frozen or fresh peas
2	cups pea tendrils

1. Whisk the eggs in a medium bowl and season with salt and pepper. Mix in the crumbled goat cheese and set aside.

2. Melt the butter in a medium sauté pan over medium heat. Add the shallots, scallions, and peas, and sauté for 2 to 3 minutes, being careful not to burn the shallots. Add the pea tendrils and cook until soft, about 4 minutes.

3. Add the egg mixture and cook for 5 minutes over low heat, leaving it undisturbed. Cover and cook for an additional 8 to 10 minutes, or until the top of the frittata is firm.

anna getty's easy green organic

open-faced avocado cheese melt

SERVES 2

There is a wonderful English teahouse in Los Angeles called Paddington's. They serve tea, scones, chicken potpies, and the most scrumptious open-faced avocado Gouda melt. Here is my version, sprinkled with a pinch of truffle salt. It makes a wonderful lunch or light dinner accompanied by side salad.

1. Slather the mayonnaise on the bread slices, about ½ teaspoon per slice. Lay the avocado slices neatly on each bread slice. Arrange the cheese on top of the avocado. Sprinkle the paprika, truffle salt, and pepper on top of the cheese.

2. Toast the sandwiches in a toaster oven set to 350 degrees F or under the broiler set on low for about 5 minutes, or until the cheese is melted.

1 teaspoon mayonnaise, or to taste

2 slices country bread

1 avocado, pitted, peeled, and thinly sliced

3 ounces cheddar or Gouda, sliced (about 4 to 6 slices)

Pinch of paprika

Truffle salt to taste

Pinch of pepper

grilled manchego cheese sandwiches with fresh tomato spread

SERVES 2

The summer I spent in Barcelona, I ate a lot of manchego cheese with fresh, crusty bread smeared with fresh tomato paste. It was a traveling student's meal, cheap and easy. Those student days inspired this grown-up grilled cheese recipe. Don't worry if you can't find organic manchego; European law prohibits any antibiotics and growth hormones in commercially sold dairy products.

½ cup chopped fresh tomatoes

1 teaspoon olive oil

⅛ teaspoon salt

Pepper to taste

Four ¾-inch-thick slices country bread

3 ounces manchego cheese, thinly sliced (6 slices; see Cook's Notes)

4 fresh basil leaves

4 teaspoons olive tapenade

Butter for grilling

1. With a mortar and pestle, mash together the tomatoes, olive oil, salt, and pepper until a chunky puree forms.

2. Spread the tomato puree onto 2 slices of the bread. Top with the cheese slices. Lay 2 basil leaves per sandwich on top of the cheese layer. Spread a thin layer of olive tapenade on the remaining 2 slices of bread. Place the bread facedown onto the basil leaves.

3. Heat a grill pan over medium-low heat, melt a small pat of butter, and add the sandwiches, weighting each one with a small pot lid. Cook for 2 to 3 minutes on each side, being careful not to burn them. Slice the sandwiches in half and serve.

COOK'S NOTES: *Manchego is Spain's most famous cheese. It's made from sheep's milk, and is usually aged from six to eighteen months. I like to go for the six-month-old cheese because it melts nicely. If you can't find manchego, go for goat cheddar.*

If you don't have a grill pan, use a regular heavy-bottomed frying pan.

pasta fresca

SERVES 6

There is nothing, and I mean nothing, like a great bowl of pasta. Something about those carbohydrates drives us crazy. We eat a lot of pasta in my house, and I rely on quick, easy recipes. This recipe is from my family friend Rosanna, who lives in the tiny village of Orgia in Tuscany, Italy. Although she doesn't own a restaurant, people travel for days just to taste her cooking. I turn to her for simple yet exquisite dishes. The no-cook aspect of the sauce makes it a hit with the novice cook and the career woman. It's tasty topped with a lot of red pepper flakes, so serve a bowl of them on the side for those who like it spicy.

	5 to 6 plum tomatoes, cut into 1⁄4-inch cubes
	5 to 6 ounces Parmesan cheese, roughly cut into 1⁄4-inch cubes
1⁄2	cup toasted pine nuts
1⁄4	cup finely chopped red onion
1⁄2	bunch fresh basil, stemmed and coarsely chopped (about 1⁄2 cup)
1⁄2	teaspoon red pepper flakes
3	tablespoons good-quality olive oil
	Salt and pepper to taste
1	pound penne pasta

1. Combine the tomatoes, Parmesan, pine nuts, onion, basil, red pepper flakes, and olive oil in a large serving bowl. Mix well and season with salt and pepper. Let stand at room temperature so the flavors develop while you prepare the pasta.

2. Fill a large pot with plenty of water. Bring to a boil over high heat and add a small handful of salt. Add the pasta and cook until al dente, still slightly firm to the bite. Before draining the pasta, remove 1 cup of cooking water and reserve.

3. Drain the pasta and transfer it to the large serving bowl with the tomato mixture. Season with salt and pepper and mix well. If the pasta seems a little dry, add some of the reserved water. Serve immediately.

simple tomato sauce and spaghetti

SERVES 4 TO 6

The first thing I ever learned to cook was the pasta dish my grand-mother taught me. It requires only four ingredients (not including the salt, pepper, and Parmesan). For years it was my staple recipe and I never revealed her secret: a stick of butter.

One 28-ounce can whole peeled tomatoes

½ cup (1 stick) unsalted butter

4 large fresh basil leaves

Salt and pepper to taste

1 pound spaghetti

1 cup freshly grated Parmesan cheese

1. Put the tomatoes in a medium sauté pan over medium heat. Use a potato masher to mash the tomatoes into coarse pieces. Add the butter and basil and simmer for 20 to 25 minutes, stirring occasionally. Season with salt and pepper.

2. Fill a large pot with plenty of water. Bring to a boil over high heat and add a small handful of salt. Add the pasta and cook until al dente, still slightly firm to the bite. Before draining the spaghetti, remove 1 cup of cooking water and reserve.

3. In a large bowl, toss the drained spaghetti with the sauce. Add some pasta water if the sauce is too dry, but don't make it watery; the sauce should hug the noodles. Mix in generous amounts of Parmesan and serve.

fusilli with toasted walnuts, olives, capers, toasted bread crumbs, and pecorino

SERVES 6

My mom sent me this recipe. It sounded unusual, but it has become my favorite pasta dish of the moment. (Although my mother is German, she is obsessed with Italian food.) With a variety of flavors and textures, the dish tastes great served hot or at room temperature. It is not a saucy sauce, so you may want to add more olive oil at the end if the sauce is too dry.

⅓	cup plus 2 tablespoons olive oil
1	cup coarsely chopped walnuts
2	garlic cloves
½	teaspoon red pepper flakes
½	cup plain dry bread crumbs
½	cup black olives, pitted and halved
2	tablespoons capers, drained
6 to 8	stems fresh flat-leaf parsley, stemmed and minced
½	cup finely grated Pecorino cheese
1	pound fusilli or farfalle pasta
	Salt and pepper to taste

1. Heat a medium sauté pan over medium heat. Add 2 tablespoons of the olive oil and then add the walnuts and garlic and cook, stirring constantly, for about 5 minutes, being careful not to let the walnuts blacken. Add the red pepper flakes and bread crumbs and cook, stirring, for 1 to 2 minutes. Add the olives and capers and remove from the heat. Add the parsley and Pecorino cheese. Set aside.

2. Fill a large pot with plenty of water. Bring to a boil over high heat and add a small handful of salt. Add the pasta and cook until al dente, still slightly firm to the bite. Drain the pasta.

3. In a large bowl mix together the pasta and the walnut mixture and stir well. Add the remaining ⅓ cup of olive oil to the pasta and mix well. Season with salt and pepper. If the pasta seems too dry, go ahead and add a little more olive oil.

glass noodle stir-fry

SERVES 6 TO 8

My mom, for someone who always said that cooking is a thankless job, cooks often. Her dishes taste wonderful. She may be a reluctant cook, but everything she prepares is a home run, including her noodle stir-fry. Her version is quite simple, but I've added a few more vegetables for color and variety. I like mung bean noodles for their clear, glasslike quality and their ability to hold their shape, but in a pinch you can substitute rice noodles, which are opaque. They are both readily available.

Heat the sesame oil in a wok or a large sauté pan over high heat. Add the garlic and ginger and cook for 1 minute, stirring constantly. Add the shiitakes, snap peas, and carrots and cook until the shiitakes are soft, 6 to 8 minutes. Add the noodles, soy sauce, and toasted sesame oil and cook for 1 minute, stirring constantly and briskly. Add the cilantro and black sesame seeds and stir until mixed. Serve immediately.

¼ cup sesame oil

1 tablespoon minced garlic

2 teaspoons minced ginger

2½ ounces shiitake mushrooms, stemmed and thinly sliced

1 cup snap peas, sliced on a diagonal

1 cup carrots, peeled and grated on large holes

4 cups mung bean noodles, soaked in hot water for 10 minutes

¼ cup soy sauce

1 tablespoon toasted sesame oil

2 tablespoons chopped fresh cilantro

1 tablespoon black sesame seeds

seared bay scallops with orzo and sun-dried tomato cream sauce

SERVES 6

The sun-dried tomato sauce is an adaptation of a recipe taught to me by my first boss, chef Darra Crouch. Marsala wine, a fortified wine from Italy, is what gives the dish such a robust flavor. Bay scallops are tiny, so do your best to sear them evenly. U.S. bay scallops suffer from depletion, so choose farm-raised bay scallops. Avoid Calico scallops.

12	ounces orzo
2	tablespoons unsalted butter
1	pound bay scallops
	Salt to taste
	Sun-Dried Tomato Cream Sauce (recipe follows)
1	tablespoon thinly sliced fresh basil

1. Cook the orzo in a pot of salted boiling water until cooked through. Drain and set aside.

2. Heat a large sauté pan over medium heat and melt the butter. Add the scallops and sauté for about 5 minutes, until they are lightly browned. Season with salt.

3. Stir all but ½ cup of the sauce into the cooked orzo. Mix well. Spoon the orzo onto individual plates and mound each bed of orzo with an equal amount of scallops. Drizzle with the remaining ½ cup of sauce. Top with the basil.

sun-dried tomato cream sauce

MAKES ABOUT 2 CUPS

1. Melt the butter in a small pot over medium heat. Add the shallot and sauté until translucent, about 2 minutes. Add the Marsala and cook until the liquid has reduced by half, about 2 minutes. Add the saffron and sun-dried tomato paste and stir.

2. Add the cream and lower the heat. Cook for 15 to 20 minutes, stirring occasionally, until the sauce has thickened slightly.

1	tablespoon unsalted butter
1	large shallot, minced
½	cup Marsala wine
⅛	teaspoon saffron threads or powder
2	tablespoons concentrated sun-dried tomato paste
1½	cups heavy cream

steamed halibut with greek salad salsa

SERVES 6

As a young woman, I spent an entire summer bartending on a small island in Greece. Every day before work I would sit at the bar and eat a Greek salad. I was obsessed with the flavor combination of feta cheese, olives, red onions, tomatoes, and oregano. Not only is the salad delicious on its own, I also find it to be the perfect topping for this steamed halibut. I also added capers for extra flavor.

1. Make the salsa. In a medium bowl, mix together the tomatoes, capers, onion, cheese, olives, thyme, olive oil, and salt and pepper. Set aside.

2. Spray a collapsible steaming rack with cooking spray and place 2 halibut fillets on the rack, skin-side down. Sprinkle the fillets with salt and pepper.

3. In a medium pot, bring the wine, peppercorns, whole basil leaves, and 1 cup of water to a boil. Lay the rack with the fillets in the pot, cover, and steam the fish for 9 to 10 minutes. Gently transfer the steamed halibut fillets to a plate and cover with a domed lid to keep warm. Repeat the process 2 more times to cook the remaining fillets.

4. Serve the steamed halibut on individual plates with Greek salsa on top or on the side. Garnish with the ribbons of basil.

1½ cups seeded and finely chopped tomatoes (about 3 plum tomatoes)

2 tablespoons capers, drained and coarsely chopped

3 tablespoons finely chopped red onion

¾ cup cubed feta cheese (¼-inch cubes)

12 Greek olives, pitted and finely chopped

1 teaspoon minced fresh thyme

1 tablespoon olive oil

Salt and pepper to taste

Six 8-ounce halibut fillets

1 cup white wine

10 whole peppercorns

6 whole fresh basil leaves, plus 4 leaves, thinly sliced, for garnish

did you know...

Polychlorinated biphenyl (PCB), an industrial chemical that has been banned in the United States for decades, is commonly found in farm-raised salmon. Farm-raised salmon account for most of the salmon supply in the United States. They are fed ground-up fish that absorb PCBs, which persist in our streams, lakes, and oceans. The problem is compounded because farmed salmon have a fish diet that is rich in fat, and PCBs are absorbed more easily through fat. (Farmed salmon contain 52 percent more fat than wild salmon, according to the U.S. Department of Agriculture.) When eating farmed salmon, trim the fat from the salmon and drain off any fat from cooking to lower the risk of ingesting PCBs.

Some fish farms claim they use fish meal made from fish that come from clean water, so their salmon contain lower levels of PCBs. That sort of claim may be worth investigating. Always go for wild-caught salmon. If not available, choose a more sustainable option.

barbecue baked alaskan salmon

SERVES 6

This is probably one of the easiest recipes in my repertoire. It couldn't be simpler: Open a jar of barbecue sauce, pour it over salmon fillets, and bake. It's great with Sautéed Fresh Corn with Cilantro and Scallions (page 187) and Garlicky Baby Bok Choy (page 183). Go for wild-caught Alaskan salmon, even if it has been frozen. It is your most sustainable choice. The difference in the flavor of wild salmon as compared to farmed is noticeable as well. Be sure to avoid barbecue sauce made with high-fructose corn syrup.

Six 8-ounce Alaskan salmon fillets

2½ cups barbecue sauce

Salt and pepper to taste

1. Preheat the oven to 350 degrees F. Spray a baking pan with nonstick cooking spray.

2. Lay the salmon fillets, skin-side down, on the baking pan. Pour the barbecue sauce over the salmon, making sure each piece is completely covered. Season with salt and pepper.

3. Bake the salmon for 15 to 20 minutes, until cooked through but still tender. (Test with a knife; the meat should be somewhat firm and the juices should run clear.) Carefully transfer to a serving platter.

double lemon chicken breasts with fresh tomato basil salsa

SERVES 4 TO 8

While I was pregnant with my daughter, India, we spent the entire summer in Italy. My husband and I took a two-week intensive immersion language class, and one day during a lunch break we came upon a tiny family-owned trattoria called Da Dino ("At Dino's"). It was nothing fancy, just two old ladies cooking simple Italian fare. True to the cravings of a pregnant woman, I ate the lemon chicken breast with a side of garlic spinach every day for those two weeks. In this recipe I serve the lemon chicken with a garlicky tomato salsa instead, called *checca* in Italian. The key to this dish is using thinly sliced chicken breasts, so ask your butcher to fillet each chicken breast half into 2 or 3 pieces, if possible.

tomato basil salsa

5	plum tomatoes, seeded and cut into ¼-inch cubes
5	large fresh basil leaves, thinly sliced
1	tablespoon minced garlic
2	tablespoons olive oil
	Pinch of salt
	Pinch of pepper

lemon chicken

¾	cup all-purpose flour
1	tablespoon grated lemon zest
	Salt and pepper to taste
8	skinless boneless chicken breast fillets, pounded until ½ inch thick
	Grapeseed or canola oil for cooking
2 to 3 lemons, halved	

1. To make the salsa, combine all of the ingredients in a bowl and mix well. Set aside.

2. To prepare the chicken, combine the flour, lemon zest, and salt and pepper on a flat dinner plate. Using a fork, mix together until thoroughly combined.

3. Wash the chicken breasts and pat them dry. Dredge each fillet in the flour mixture, making sure to coat both sides. Set aside.

4. Heat a large sauté pan over medium heat and add the grapeseed oil, using just enough to coat the bottom of the pan. Add the chicken fillets in batches, cooking each side until lightly golden (about 2 minutes per side). Before removing the chicken from the pan, squeeze generous amounts of lemon juice over each piece. Serve topped with the basil salsa.

green tip

Go for free-range certified organic chicken that is free of antibiotics, hormones, and artificial ingredients. Plus no herbicides or pesticides are used in their feed. They are also treated more humanely while alive.

coconut chicken curry over basmati rice with almonds and raisins

SERVES 6

In Ayurveda, the ancient healing philosophy of India, there are six key tastes: sweet, salty, sour, pungent, bitter, and astringent. All of these elements are represented in this beautiful curry. This dish can be served with a simple green salad and is filling enough to be a complete meal. The sweetness of the raisins adds such a lovely balance to the spicy curry chicken.

1. To prepare the chicken, heat the vegetable oil in a large sauté pan over medium-high heat. Add the onion and cook for 5 minutes. Add the mustard seeds and cook for 2 minutes. Stir in the garlic, ginger, cumin, coriander, and curry powder. Add the chicken and cook, stirring constantly, for about 7 minutes, or until cooked through. Lower the heat, add the yogurt, and stir until mixed thoroughly.

2. To make the rice, combine 3 cups of water, the rice, raisins, and cardamom in a medium pot and bring to a boil. Cover, lower the heat, and simmer until the water is absorbed, 12 to 15 minutes. Remove from the heat and let the rice sit with the lid on for a few minutes. Transfer to a bowl and mix in the almonds, cilantro, and salt.

3. Serve the curry chicken over the basmati rice on a large serving platter or on individual plates.

COOK'S NOTE: *If slivered almonds are not readily available, you can substitute raw cashew halves. Cashews taste and look great and are actually quite common in Indian dishes.*

coconut curry chicken

2	tablespoons vegetable oil
1	large yellow onion, cut in half, and then sliced ¼ inch thick
2	teaspoons mustard seeds
2	teaspoons minced garlic
2	teaspoons minced ginger
1½	teaspoons ground cumin
1½	teaspoons ground coriander
1½	tablespoons curry powder
4	skinless boneless chicken breast halves (about 1¾ pounds), cut into ½-inch strips
1½	cups plain yogurt

rice

1½	cups basmati rice, rinsed
½	cup raisins
5	cardamom pods
½	cup slivered almonds (see Cook's Note)
3	tablespoons coarsely chopped fresh cilantro
	Salt to taste

"green" salt

A good cook needs very few essential items in the kitchen—a good knife, a sturdy pot, and a little pot of salt. While salt is a crucial element in almost every dish, it wasn't always relegated to the kitchen. In past centuries, it has been used as a form of currency, as part of religious rituals, and as a preservative. The power of these tiny white crystals is astonishing. We literally can't live without salt or sodium; it is a mineral that your body cannot produce on its own.

Using the word "organic" with salt is tricky because salt cannot be organically grown; it is a mineral, not a plant. However, there are countries that regulate salt labels to ensure that the product is harvested by hand without harming the environment and without purifying the salt (altering it chemically) in any way. Right now only three countries have this certification: New Zealand, Wales, and France. Bio-Gro is New Zealand's seal for organic salt, while Wales has a Soil Association certified stamp for its organic salt. France's Nature & Progrés label is given to salt that is harvested and produced according to organic methods and standards, which means the salt is unprocessed and all-natural. The label guarantees that the salt was harvested with nonpolluting tools from an unpolluted environment free of pesticides and other contaminants. There are several French brands that are certified in this manner.

One specialty salt certified by France's Nature & Progrés is fleur de sel. This type of sea salt is harvested on the coast of Brittany, in France. It has different flavors, depending on the exact location where it is harvested. The fleur de sel from the town of Guérande is the most prized; some call it the Champagne of salts. Fleur de sel is most often used as a finishing salt because its flavor stands out best when it is left uncooked.

New Zealand is a wonderful source for sea salt. Much of it is harvested in the Cook Strait, which separates the North and South Islands as well as the Southern Ocean. Many salt producers in New Zealand claim to have the purest salts because the water is free of pollutants. Some of the salt is cream colored because of the natural mineral content in the water.

Wales is known for its sea salt, harvested from the Atlantic Ocean. Halen Môn is the best-known brand of Welsh salt, and it is certified by the Soil Association.

I am a salt addict and am constantly looking for unique salts from artisans. By buying artisanal salt, you're supporting the salt farmers and artisans of the world.

garden herb and garlic clay pot chicken

SERVES 4 TO 6

In our early years together, my husband always talked about his famous clay pot chicken. It became a joke in our household as the years passed, as he never made the chicken. Finally, on my thirty-third birthday, he surprised me with a beautifully roasted clay pot chicken he had spent the day preparing. This recipe is dedicated to him. The clay pot I use is a medium-size Siena clay pot with a lid. You can also use a small roasting pan and cover the chicken with recycled aluminum foil. I do encourage you to go online and purchase a clay pot if you cannot find one locally. It really retains the flavor of the chicken while it roasts.

One 4- to 5-pound chicken

4 tablespoons unsalted butter, at room temperature

1 tablespoon minced fresh sage

1 tablespoon minced fresh rosemary

1 tablespoon minced fresh basil

2 tablespoons minced garlic

¼ teaspoon salt

2 lemons, halved

Freshly cracked pepper to taste

1. Soak the clay pot top and bottom in cold water for 30 minutes. Wash the chicken and pat it dry.

2. In a small bowl, mix together the butter, sage, rosemary, basil, garlic, and salt. Using your hands, spread the herb butter all over the chicken: inside the cavity, under the skin, and in all the nooks and crannies.

3. Place the chicken in the clay pot bottom. Squeeze the lemons over the chicken and then stuff the rinds into the cavity. Season the chicken generously with cracked pepper.

4. Put the lid on the pot and place it in a cold oven on the middle rack. Turn the oven to 475 degrees F. Bake the chicken for 1 hour and 15 minutes. Remove the lid and baste the chicken, and bake for another 10 minutes, or until it is nice and brown and the juices run clear when the thigh is pierced with a knife.

5. Serve hot with sides of your choice.

turkey sausage with red peppers and hazelnut brown rice

SERVES 4

With the turkey sausage, brown rice, and hazelnuts, you have a protein-packed meal. It's a perfect winter dish, a crowd-pleaser, and it is pretty too. Look for nitrate-free turkey sausage.

1	cup brown rice
½	cup chopped hazelnuts
2	tablespoons unsalted butter
	Salt to taste
¼	cup chopped fresh flat-leaf parsley, plus additional for garnish
2	tablespoons grapeseed oil
½	teaspoon red pepper flakes
1	medium yellow onion, cut into ¼-inch strips
½	medium-large red bell pepper, cut into 2-inch matchsticks
4	turkey sausages (about 1 pound)

1. Put the rice in a small saucepan with 2 cups of water. Bring to a boil, cover, and simmer for 40 to 50 minutes. Remove from the heat and let stand, covered.

2. Toast the hazelnuts in a dry medium saucepan over medium heat, stirring constantly, until browned, about 5 minutes. (Be careful not to burn the nuts.) Add the butter and cook until the butter is lightly browned, 1 to 2 minutes. Add the rice, salt, and the ¼ cup of parsley and cook for another 4 to 5 minutes, stirring constantly. Remove from the heat, cover, and set aside.

3. Heat the grapeseed oil in a large sauté pan over medium-high heat. Add the red pepper flakes, onion, and bell pepper and cook for 5 to 7 minutes. Add the sausages and cook until browned, 3 to 4 minutes on each side. (Remove the onion and bell pepper if they look like they are about to burn.)

4. Mound the rice on a large serving platter and top with the sausages. Scatter the onion and bell peppers over the top and garnish with the remaining chopped parsley.

paul's filet mignon with whiskey cream sauce

SERVES 6

I very rarely eat beef but when I do, this is it. My dear Irish friend Paul Barnett learned how to make this steak while working in a French restaurant in Ireland. What sets this dish apart is the pink Himalayan salt used to coat the fillets. While it sounds exotic, the salt is widely available in supermarkets and online. If not available, use another coarse mineral salt. The sauce is similar to the sauce for the classic dish, steak *au poivre* ("with pepper"). This one is peppery and creamy and oh so good.

Six	6-ounce filet mignons
1½	tablespoons salt, preferably Himalayan
2	tablespoons crushed peppercorns
½	cup Irish whiskey
½	cup heavy cream

1. Coat the steaks with the salt and pepper 30 minutes before cooking.

2. Heat a large dry sauté pan over medium-high heat. Place the steaks in the hot pan and sear them for 2 minutes. Flip them over and sear the second side for 2 minutes. Continue flipping the steaks over every 2 minutes until cooked to the desired level of doneness, about 10 minutes for medium-rare. Transfer the steaks to a serving plate.

3. Carefully pour the whiskey into the pan and ignite it with a match. Be sure to stand back. Once the alcohol has burned off, add the cream and whisk the sauce. When the sauce has browned, pour it over the steaks and serve.

did you know. . .

Himalayan sea salt is the purest of salts, is uncontaminated by pollutants and toxins, and is rich in 84 minerals (see Resources, page 243).

anna getty's easy green organic

did you know...

In 2007 there were 21 major episodes in the United States involving beef products contaminated by *E. coli*, up from just 6 episodes in 2005. Several factors are thought to explain the dramatic increase: Perhaps a more virulent strain of the bacterium has emerged. Maybe the heat wave in the summer of 2007 increased the stress level of the cows. Or bacteria is getting into the distillers' grain (a by-product of ethanol production), which is fed to cows. Organic beef cattle are finished on pasture and grass-based forage instead of corn, which reduces stress on the animal and the frequency of *E. coli*.

Cloning is another issue related to beef. Just think—you might be one of several thousand Americans who have already consumed meat from a cloned cow or bull, or the progeny of a cloned animal. Don't bother to ask if your meat market is selling products from cloned animals. The odds are they won't know, since the U.S. Food and Drug Administration has determined there is no need or justification for labeling cloned meat, but the jury is still out on long-term effects of eating meat from cloned animals. The only way to avoid cloned animal products is to look for the U.S. Department of Agriculture organic seal.

CHAPTER

6

side dishes

The side dish should complement the main course. While the main course often gets the most attention, the side dish is the supporting player, accenting the main event but holding its own on the plate. Think of the flavors and colors on the plate when choosing a side dish; avoid flavor clashes by choosing one strong flavor or theme to guide the meal. For example, if the main course has a strong flavor, such as Coconut Chicken Curry over Basmati Rice with Almonds and Raisins (page 170), choose a subtle, delicate vegetable to pair with it, like Sautéed Baby Squash with Tarragon and Soy Sauce (page 184).

The most important thing to remember when preparing side dishes is to use fresh, local, and seasonal produce. Vegetable side dishes like Sautéed Swiss Chard with Garlic, Raisins, and Pine Nuts (page 181), John Pepper's Exotic Green Beans (page 189), and Maple-Orange Glazed Carrots (page 185) show that it's easy to add vegetables to your diet by finding creative ways to cook them.

belgian endive and fennel gratin

SERVES 4 TO 6

In France, Belgian endive gratin is as common a side dish as mashed potatoes are in the United States. The gratin is almost always served alongside a meat dish, but can be part of a vegetarian entrée. The anise flavor of the fennel and the slightly bitter endive are mellowed with a little cheese and heavy cream.

6	Belgian endive, halved, root ends intact
3	fennel bulbs, halved crosswise
1	cup Chicken Stock (page 112)
2	tablespoons salted butter, cut into ¼-inch pieces
	Juice of 1 lemon
1	tablespoon sugar
2	tablespoons heavy cream
1	cup finely grated Swiss cheese
½	cup plain dry bread crumbs

1. Place the endive and fennel, cut-sides down, in a heavy-bottomed pot or Dutch oven. Add the stock, butter, lemon juice, and sugar.

2. Trace the lid of the pot on a sheet of recycled parchment paper and cut it out with scissors. Butter one side of the parchment circle. (The parchment paper will help cook the endive and fennel.) Place the paper circle, buttered-side down, on top of the endive and fennel and put the lid on the pot. Simmer, covered, for 20 to 30 minutes, until the endive and fennel are fork-tender.

3. Preheat the oven to 450 degrees F. Butter a gratin dish just large enough for the endive and fennel to lay flat in a single layer.

4. With a slotted spoon, transfer the endive and fennel to the gratin dish and pour the cream over the top. Mix the cheese and bread crumbs together in a small bowl and sprinkle the mixture evenly over the endive and fennel.

5. Bake the gratin for 10 minutes, or until the top is golden and bubbly.

anna getty's easy green organic

sautéed swiss chard with garlic, raisins, and pine nuts

SERVES 2 TO 4

Swiss chard is a sophisticated green, a step up from ordinary spinach. (The plant is actually a beet bred for its leaves.) Whether you choose red, yellow, or green, Swiss chard is so versatile. There are endless ways to prepare it; you can sauté it with a little garlic, for example, or add a handful to a casserole or to bean soups. I even put it in my green smoothies sometimes. This healthful and hearty side dish has a slight kick to it because of the red pepper flakes and a sweetness because of the raisins. It makes a lovely accompaniment to the Double Lemon Chicken Breasts with Fresh Tomato Basil Salsa (page 169).

2	bunches red Swiss chard (about 30 leaves)
2	tablespoons canola oil
2	garlic cloves, smashed and peeled
½	teaspoon anise seeds
½	teaspoon fennel seeds
⅓	teaspoon red pepper flakes
½	cup raisins, soaked in water overnight and drained; ½ cup pine nuts
	Salt to taste
1	tablespoon olive oil for drizzling

1. Trim the stalks off the leaves of Swiss chard. Cut the leaves into ½-inch-wide strips and wash them. (It's not necessary to dry them because the water will help cook the chard.)

2. Heat a large sauté pan over high heat and add the canola oil. Add the garlic, anise seeds, fennel seeds, red pepper flakes, and raisins. Cook, stirring, for 1 to 2 minutes and add the chard. Sauté until slightly wilted, 3 to 4 minutes. Stir in the pine nuts.

3. Turn off the heat, season the chard with salt, and drizzle with the olive oil.

green tip

After boiling eggs or steaming vegetables, let the water cool and use it to water your plants.

roasted baby beets with horseradish cream and walnuts

SERVES 6

I never enjoyed beets when I was growing up. Much like capers and goat cheese, beets were an acquired taste for me, but now I can't get enough of them. I love to juice them, roast them, steam them, and eat them raw in salads. Known for their liver-cleansing properties, beets are also high in vitamins A and C and are rich in folate. This dish goes along perfectly with Paul's Filet Mignon with Whiskey Cream Sauce (page 174).

16	red and yellow baby beets, tops and tails trimmed
2	tablespoons freshly grated or prepared horseradish
3	tablespoons sour cream
3	tablespoons plain yogurt
1	tablespoon Champagne vinegar
1	tablespoon Dijon mustard
	Salt and pepper to taste
½	cup coarsely chopped walnuts
2	teaspoons minced fresh chives

1. Steam the beets in a covered steamer insert set over simmering water until fork-tender, about 30 minutes. Replenish the water in the pot if it cooks off quickly. Remove the beets and let them cool.

2. Peel the beets with your hands under cold running water (the skins will slip off easily). Yes, your hands may turn pink; rinse them with lemon juice later to remove the color, or just wear gloves while peeling. Cut the beets in half.

3. In a small bowl, mix together the horseradish, sour cream, yogurt, vinegar, mustard, and salt and pepper. Pour the dressing over the beets and mix until they are well coated. Add the walnuts and chives and stir until well blended.

garlicky baby bok choy

SERVES 4 TO 6

Found frequently in Chinese dishes, bok choy is a type of cabbage that tastes a little like spinach. The freshest bok choy will have dark green leaves and firm white stalks, free of brown spots. You should have no trouble finding baby bok choy year-round, but large bok choy will also work well; substitute 1 large bunch for the 4 small ones called for.

4	small bunches bok choy
1	tablespoon sunflower or canola oil
2	garlic cloves, minced
1	tablespoon tamari or soy sauce
1	teaspoon toasted sesame oil
1½	teaspoons toasted sesame seeds
	Salt to taste

1. Chop the bok choy crosswise into ½-inch strips and wash thoroughly.

2. Heat a medium sauté pan or wok over medium heat. Add the sunflower oil and then the garlic. Cook, stirring briskly, for 30 to 60 seconds, being careful not to burn the garlic. Add the bok choy and cook, stirring frequently, until soft, about 5 minutes. Add the tamari and sesame oil and stir. Add the sesame seeds and salt to taste and stir again. Serve hot.

sautéed baby squash with tarragon and soy sauce

SERVES 4 TO 6

Squash are the defining vegetable of summer. Yellow and green squash seem to overtake the garden and the supermarket. Squash blossoms are the best part of the bounty. When you can find them, these bright orange flowers lend a subtle, earthy flavor to a dish. Look for squash blossoms at your local farmers' market or ask your local specialty grocer to order them for you. In this dish the rather neutral flavor of squash is brought to life with a dash of tamari and fresh tarragon. This dish is still great even if you can't find squash blossoms.

- 1 tablespoon grapeseed oil
- 1½ pounds mixed baby squash, stemmed
- 2 tablespoons tamari or soy sauce
- 1 tablespoon finely chopped fresh tarragon, plus leaves for garnish
- 8-10 squash blossoms, cut into ribbons

Heat a large sauté pan over medium heat and add the oil. Add the squash and cook, stirring constantly, for 5 minutes. Add the tamari and 1 tablespoon of water and cook for another 5 minutes. Add the tarragon and squash blossoms and cook for an additional 5 minutes. Transfer the squash to a serving dish and garnish with the tarragon leaves.

maple-orange glazed carrots

SERVES 4 TO 6

These glorious orange carrots are the perfect holiday side dish, but you can enjoy them year-round. I love their sweetness, and they're popular among sugar-crazed children, as well.

1. Preheat the oven to 425 degrees F.

2. Combine the carrots, thyme, and cinnamon in a baking dish.

3. Combine the butter, orange juice, orange zest, maple syrup, and brown sugar in a bowl and mix well. Pour the mixture over the carrots and bake until tender, stirring occasionally so that the carrots do not brown too much on one side, 1 hour to 1 hour and 15 minutes.

6	carrots, peeled and cut into 2-inch sticks
6	sprigs fresh thyme
2	cinnamon sticks
3	tablespoons unsalted butter, melted
1/3	cup fresh orange juice
1	teaspoon grated orange zest
5	tablespoons maple syrup
1	tablespoon brown sugar

sautéed fresh corn with cilantro and scallions

SERVES 4 TO 6

The key to this dish is the fresh corn. Thawed frozen corn will work too, but there is something about the clean taste and pleasing texture of freshly husked corn that makes it worth waiting for corn to hit the market. I love this with Barbecue Baked Alaskan Salmon (page 167). The combination is an unbeatable way to celebrate the Fourth of July.

2	tablespoons unsalted butter
5	cups fresh corn kernels (about 6 ears of corn)
¼	cup chopped fresh cilantro
¼	cup chopped scallions (white and green parts)
	Salt and pepper to taste

Melt the butter in a medium or large sauté pan over medium heat. Add the corn and cook for 5 minutes, stirring frequently. Add the cilantro and scallions and mix well and season with salt and pepper. Serve warm or at room temperature.

did you know. . .

A variety of genetically modified corn that was approved for human consumption in 2006 caused signs of liver disease and kidney toxicity as well as hormonal changes in rats, according to a study performed by the Committee for Independent Research and Genetic Engineering at the University of Caen in France.

john pepper's exotic green beans

SERVES 4 TO 6

I used to babysit for John Pepper's two young children when I lived in Paris many years ago. One day I found a plastic container of these miraculous cooked green beans in the refrigerator. I tasted them and was blown away, and John was happy to share the recipe. The ingredients list is long, but these are the best green beans you'll ever make.

Heat a medium sauté pan over medium heat. When the pan is hot, add the oil, garlic, onion, and bay leaves and cook for 5 to 6 minutes, until the garlic and onion is lightly browned but not burned. Add the wine (if using) and cook until the liquid has evaporated. Add the paprika, cumin, coriander, and curry powder and mix well. Add the raisins and mix well again. Add the butter and green beans and stir until the butter has melted. Add the crème fraîche, almonds, and cilantro. Season with the salt and pepper.

1	tablespoon canola oil
2	garlic cloves, sliced
½	medium yellow or white onion, finely diced
3	bay leaves
⅓	cup white wine (optional)
1	teaspoon paprika
1	teaspoon ground cumin
1	teaspoon ground coriander
½	teaspoon curry powder
1	cup golden raisins, soaked for at least 2 hours or overnight, and drained
3	tablespoons unsalted butter
1	pound green beans, cooked until crisp-tender
½	cup crème fraîche or sour cream
¼	cup sliced almonds
⅓	cup finely chopped fresh cilantro
	Salt and freshly cracked pepper to taste

did you know. . .

Twenty-six percent of the 548 green bean samples tested in 2004 by the U.S. Department of Agriculture (USDA) contained 3 or more insecticide residues, and 14 samples contained 5 or more residues. Green beans had the highest Dietary Risk Index (DRI) score of any domestically grown vegetable tested in recent years by the USDA: 330. Residues of relatively high-risk organophosphate insecticides pushed up the DRI score for this crop. Imported green beans scored lower on the DRI: 93.

balsamic-broiled asparagus with shaved parmesan cheese

SERVES 4 TO 6

Asparagus stands tall and noble like a spire and is the first sign of spring. Rich in vitamin A and phosphorus, it has been deemed the "aristocrat of vegetables" by the people of Quebec. Although steaming asparagus is the most popular way to cook it, I love grilling or broiling it as well. If the asparagus stems are thin, it's not necessary to trim too much off the bottoms. For thicker asparagus, trim off about 2 inches.

1½ pounds asparagus, trimmed

2 tablespoons balsamic vinegar

¼ cup olive oil

Salt and pepper to taste

One 2-ounce piece Parmesan cheese

1. Preheat the broiler.

2. Lay the asparagus in a single layer in a large gratin dish.

3. In a small bowl, mix together the vinegar, olive oil, and salt and pepper. Pour the dressing over the asparagus and bake for about 20 minutes, or until tender but still firm.

4. Let the asparagus cool and then transfer it to a small platter or serving dish. Using a potato peeler, grate 6 to 8 thin pieces of Parmesan and crumble the cheese over the asparagus.

did you know. . .

In a 2002 test, only 9 percent of the domestic asparagus samples tested contained 1 pesticide residue, and less than 1 percent contained 2 or more residues. Because asparagus grows quickly and early in the growing season, pesticide residues are not a problem in the vast majority of the asparagus produced in the United States.

baked purple cauliflower with rosemary and garlic

Once you adjust to the surprising color, purple cauliflower (an heirloom variety) will become a favorite in your house. Purple cauliflower has a subtler flavor than its white cousin and gets its color from an antioxidant called anthocyanin, which is also responsible for purple grapes and red cabbage. Be careful not to overcook the cauliflower, as the rich purple will turn green. Feel free to substitute white cauliflower if you can't find purple.

4	small heads purple cauliflower, broken into florets (or use 2 medium heads white cauliflower)
3	garlic cloves, quartered
1	tablespoon coarsely chopped fresh rosemary
¼	cup olive oil
	Salt and pepper to taste
1	tablespoon coarsely chopped fresh flat-leaf parsley for garnish

1. Preheat the oven to 425 degrees F.

2. Combine the cauliflower florets, garlic, rosemary, olive oil, and salt and pepper in a medium bowl and mix well. Transfer to a large baking dish and bake for 35 to 40 minutes, until the cauliflower is browned and somewhat tender when poked with a fork.

3. Sprinkle the parsley over the cauliflower and serve warm or at room temperature.

sweet potato medallions

SERVES 4 TO 6

In my house we eat sweet potatoes every Sunday, a tradition we call Sweet Potato Sunday. We usually bake them whole and then top them with generous amounts of butter, maple syrup, and cinnamon. I like to mix it up and make these scrumptious medallions, an idea I picked up in a catering kitchen.

3	pounds garnet yams, with skin on, sliced ⅓ inch thick
¼	cup agave nectar
1	tablespoon soy sauce
1	teaspoon grated ginger or ½ teaspoon ginger powder

1. Preheat the oven to 375 degrees F. Line 2 baking sheets with parchment paper.

2. Lay the sweet potato rounds on the baking sheets. In a small bowl, mix together the agave nectar, soy sauce, and ginger. Using a pastry or basting brush, coat both sides of the medallions with the soy syrup. Bake for 30 minutes, turning them over after 15 minutes.

3. Remove the sweet potatoes from the oven and turn over each medallion. Coat the second side of each medallion with the soy syrup and bake for another 20 to 25 minutes, or until lightly browned.

sweet potato fries with maple barbecue sauce

SERVES 4 TO 6

It's tough to get my daughter to eat any type of vegetable other than corn on the cob, peas with butter, and green beans, but she just loves her Sweet Potato Fries. They are a great alternative to regular potato fries. These fries are not only packed with vitamins and minerals, they are baked instead of deep-fried. I use garnet yams for this dish for their vibrant color. The sweet potatoes are sliced thickly, like steak-cut fries.

1. Preheat the oven to 400 degrees F.

2. To make the fries, put the yams in a large bowl. In a small bowl mix together the cumin, coriander, garlic powder, paprika, olive oil, and salt. Pour the mixture over the yams. Using your hands, toss thoroughly until the yams are evenly coated. Add the parsley and mix well.

3. Arrange the yams in a single layer on a large baking sheet and bake, stirring occasionally, for about 30 minutes, or until the edges are brown and the potatoes are cooked through.

4. To make the sauce, mix the barbecue sauce and maple syrup together in a small bowl.

5. Sprinkle the fries with sea salt and serve immediately with the sauce on the side.

sweet potato fries

4	medium garnet yams, peeled and cut into ½-inch-thick strips
2	teaspoons ground cumin
2	teaspoons ground coriander
2	teaspoons garlic powder
2	teaspoons sweet paprika
½	cup olive oil
1½	teaspoons salt
2	tablespoons minced fresh flat-leaf parsley
	Sea salt for sprinkling

maple barbecue sauce

¾	cup barbecue sauce
3	tablespoons maple syrup

did you know...

Only 4.5 percent of sweet potatoes tested by the U.S. Department of Agriculture in 2003 contained 3 or more petsicide residues. Fifty percent contained 1 residue and 35 percent tested clean.

sage skillet potatoes

SERVES 4 TO 6

Almost everyone I know is a sucker for potatoes. There is something comforting about the starchy quality of them. One of my favorite meals in Germany is called *krusti*. It's essentially a large plate of skillet potatoes cooked with different vegetables and topped with two large fried eggs. With a touch of earthy sage, these skillet potatoes are perfect alongside eggs, but are also wonderful with filet mignon, chicken, or fish.

10 red-skinned new potatoes or fingerling potatoes, with skins on

2 tablespoons unsalted butter

15 small fresh sage leaves

Salt and freshly cracked pepper to taste

1. Boil the potatoes in water to cover for about 20 minutes, leaving them slightly undercooked. Drain the potatoes, let cool, and cut in half.

2. Heat a large skillet over high heat. Melt the butter and add the sage leaves. Sauté them until crisp, 3 to 4 minutes. Add the potatoes and cook them, stirring constantly, until they are lightly browned, 10 to 12 minutes.

3. Add salt and pepper to taste and serve hot.

desserts and sweets

If I could survive solely on sweets, I would, and I know I'm not alone. There's something about a sweet that completes a meal, even if it's just one bite. Desserts offer a great opportunity for you to feature seasonal fruit like berries in the summer and apples and pears in the winter, so look around your local farmers' market or supermarket and get inspired by the beauty of fresh organic fruit. But desserts shouldn't be *too* sweet; you should be able to taste all of the notes of a dessert.

This chapter includes some of my favorite desserts. You'll find Caramelized Banana Cream Pie (page 218) and dark chocolate–dipped strawberries with a twist (page 231). Whether you prefer chocolate, fruit, or something more savory, there's a sweet in here for you. I have never considered myself a baker, but I had great success developing these recipes, including a tangy Mango Bread Pudding (page 217) and crunchy Dried Cranberry and Toasted Hazelnut Macaroons (page 221), as well as "healthy" sweets like banana bread with dark chocolate chips (page 224), zucchini sweet potato bread (page 223), and Strawberry Frozen Yogurt Pie with Granola Crunch (page 210). Have fun with these recipes, and remember to treat yourself and enjoy the fruits of your labor and the chocolate, too!

dates stuffed two ways

Sweet, chewy dates are transformed into savory desserts when stuffed; the goat cheese adds a creaminess, while almond butter adds something unexpected. Considered one of the oldest cultivated fruits in the world, dates get their name from the Greek word for fingers, *daktylos*, and are the fruit of the date palm tree. I like to serve these with a pot of mint tea.

¼ cup goat cheese, at room temperature

1 teaspoon crystallized ginger, minced

20 cold Medjool dates, halved and pitted

¼ cup almond butter

1. In a small bowl, mix the goat cheese and ginger until combined.

2. Using a small spoon, spoon about ½ teaspoon of the mixture into each of 20 date halves. Fill the remaining date halves with the almond butter.

3. Refrigerate the stuffed dates for 30 minutes before serving.

figs in port wine with greek yogurt

SERVES 6

This Mediterranean-inspired dessert is one of my favorites. The figs plump up so beautifully and soak up the port. The plain Greek yogurt balances out the sweetness of the drunken figs.

18	dried Mission figs, stemmed
1	cup port
½	cup fresh orange juice
1	teaspoon grated orange zest, plus additional for garnish
4	cardamom pods
6	cloves
1	cinnamon stick
⅓	cup sugar
4	cups Greek yogurt

1. Combine the figs, port, orange juice, the 1 teaspoon of orange zest, the cardamom, cloves, cinnamon stick, and sugar in a small saucepan. Heat over low heat and simmer the figs for 40 minutes. Increase the heat to medium-high and reduce the port until it thickens slightly. (You can use a spoon to test its thickness.) Remove from the heat.

2. Allow the figs to cool to room temperature and discard the cinnamon stick, cardamom pods, and cloves.

3. Spoon about ⅔ cup of yogurt into each of 6 small bowls. Then spoon 3 figs and a bit of syrup over each serving and garnish with orange zest.

COOK'S NOTE: *If you feel like being really decadent, serve the figs over vanilla ice cream. Green and Black's makes a beautiful organic vanilla bean ice cream—yum!*

green tip

We eat a lot of yogurt in our house, so I try to buy yogurt in glass jars as often as possible. We reuse the little glass jars to mix paints and save the large ones to store grains. But most yogurt these days comes in plastic containers. Instead of throwing them away or recycling them, save them for seed starters for your garden. The plastic containers are large enough and sturdy enough to accommodate seedlings until they are ready to be transferred to a pot or garden.

berries with basil and lavender-honey yogurt drizzle

SERVES 6

I love eating and cooking with fresh berries when they are at their peak in the summer. The key to this dish is allowing the berries to macerate (marinate) in the sugar, lemon juice, lemon zest, and basil. This is a great make-ahead dish if you're in a time crunch. The basil and lavender oil add a refined touch to an otherwise very simple dessert. Remember when using essential oils, a little goes a long way. You don't want your yogurt drizzle tasting like perfume.

1	pint raspberries
1	pint blackberries or boysenberries
1	quart strawberries, hulled and halved
2	tablespoons sugar
2	tablespoons fresh lemon juice
½	teaspoon grated lemon zest
4	fresh basil leaves, thinly sliced
½	cup plain yogurt
1	tablespoon wildflower honey
2	drops lavender oil (see Cook's Note)
1	teaspoon fresh or dried lavender flowers, plus additional for garnish

1. In a large nonreactive bowl, gently mix together the raspberries, blackberries, strawberries, sugar, lemon juice and zest, and basil. Set aside to macerate for 30 minutes to 1 hour.

2. In a small bowl, mix together the yogurt, honey, lavender oil, and the 1 teaspoon of lavender flowers.

3. Divide the berries among 6 small bowls. Drizzle each serving with about 1½ tablespoons of the lavender yogurt and garnish with a lavender flower.

COOK'S NOTE: *Get creative with essential oils in the kitchen. While they're usually found in massage oils at spas, essential oils make a great flavor enhancer in certain dishes. Good organic essential oils are on the pricey side, ranging from eleven dollars to over two hundred dollars for a quarter of an ounce, but for cooking, you only want a drop or two. Essential oils are not really oil; they are the concentrated plant liquid extracted through a steam heat process. Sweet-smelling essential oils have been used for their medicinal qualities for centuries and have recently shown up in natural cleaning as well as body care products. Even chefs are starting to use them creatively in their cuisine, making sauces with basil, oregano, and thyme oil. I love adding a few drops of rose oil to whipped cream, orange oil to frostings, and lemon oil to salad dressings. Use only organic, therapeutic-grade essential oils in cooking.*

pear and blueberry crisp with brown sugar sour cream

SERVES 6

In my family I am known as the crumble queen because I specialize in fruit crumbles and crisps. Easier than making pie, crumbles and crisps let the featured fruit shine. The crispy or crumbly topping adds a little crunch and holds the sweet cream poured on top. I make endless varieties, using whatever fruit is in season. And the great thing about crisps and crumbles is that it is okay to use frozen fruit. Just make sure you thaw the fruit before baking.

1. Preheat the oven to 375 degrees F.

2. Combine the pears and lemon juice in a large bowl. Add the blueberries and mix well. Set aside.

3. Heat a large sauté pan over medium heat. Melt the 2 tablespoons of butter and add the pear and blueberry mixture, the sugar, and vanilla. Cook, stirring occasionally, for 5 to 7 minutes, until the pears just begin to soften. Transfer the mixture to an 8-by-11-inch baking dish.

4. To prepare the topping, mix together the flour, oats, brown sugar, almonds, cinnamon, nutmeg, and salt. Using your hands, begin adding the butter and work it into the flour until the mixture resembles a coarse meal.

5. Spread the topping evenly over the pears and blueberries. Bake the crisp for 30 to 35 minutes, or until the top is brown and the juices are bubbling.

6. To make the sour cream, mix together the sour cream and brown sugar until the brown sugar dissolves.

7. Serve the crisp warm, with a spoonful of the Brown Sugar Sour Cream on top.

3½ pounds Bosc pears, peeled, cored, and thinly sliced

Juice of ½ lemon

1½ cups fresh or frozen blueberries (thawed if frozen)

2 tablespoons unsalted butter

2 tablespoons sugar

2 teaspoons vanilla extract

crisp topping

1 cup unbleached all-purpose flour

½ cup quick-cooking oats

1 cup packed light brown sugar

½ cup slivered almonds

1 teaspoon ground cinnamon

½ teaspoon ground nutmeg

¼ teaspoon salt

½ cup (1 stick) cold unsalted butter, cut into ½-inch cubes

brown sugar sour cream

¾ cup sour cream

1 tablespoon light brown sugar

mini—strawberry rhubarb crumbles

These mini-crumbles are the gourmand's dessert. Perfect in size and bursting with flavor, they bring sweet strawberries and zesty rhubarb to life. This crumble is particularly delicious in early summer, when both strawberries and rhubarb are at their peak, but feel free to use frozen fruit (thawed), if fresh options are not available. I love eating these crumbles warm, with a dollop of cold whipped cream, but enjoy it topped with ice cream if you like. Or eat it plain; it will be just as good.

2	tablespoons unsalted butter
4	cups thinly sliced strawberries
1	large rib rhubarb, thinly sliced
2	tablespoons sugar
1	tablespoon fresh lemon juice

crumble topping

½	cup unbleached all-purpose flour
¼	cup packed light brown sugar
3	tablespoons cold unsalted butter, cut into pea-size pieces

1. Preheat the oven to 375 degrees F.

2. Melt the 2 tablespoons of butter in a medium saucepan over medium heat. Add the strawberries and rhubarb and cook, stirring constantly, for 2 to 3 minutes. Add the sugar and lemon juice and cook for 2 more minutes. Remove from the heat and set aside.

3. To make the topping, mix together the flour, brown sugar, and butter pieces with your hands until the mixture resembles a coarse meal.

4. Divide the fruit among 6 ramekins. Divide the topping evenly, making sure the fruit is completely covered.

5. Place the ramekins on a small baking sheet and bake for 25 to 30 minutes, until the topping is golden and bubbly. Serve warm.

did you know. . .

Forty-five percent of 731 strawberry samples tested in 2004 by the U.S. Department of Agriculture (USDA) had 3 or more pesticide residues, and 22 samples had 6 or more residues. Based on the USDA's test results for 2004 and food consumption data, Americans ate about 6 million servings of strawberries that contained 6 or more residues. Domestically grown conventional strawberries scored 56 on the Dietary Risk Index, the fourth-highest score among fruits tested in recent years by the USDA. Imported strawberries scored 78.

strawberry frozen yogurt pie with granola crunch

SERVES 6 TO 8

I designed this dessert for my daughter, India, and her friends. India is constantly asking me for ice cream, so I came up with a healthful alternative. This pie is low in sugar and fat, and high in fiber and vitamin C—and it puts a smile on a child's face.

1½ cups fresh or frozen strawberries (thawed if frozen)

½ cup agave nectar

2 cups plain yogurt

2 tablespoons soy margarine, melted

2 cups granola

1. Combine the strawberries, agave nectar, and yogurt in a blender and blend until smooth.

2. Transfer the mixture to an 8½-inch stainless-steel pie pan. Place the pie in the freezer and allow to set for 1 hour.

3. In a small bowl, mix the melted margarine with the granola. Spread the granola mixture evenly on top of the pie. Cover with aluminum foil and return to the freezer for at least 1 hour, or up to 2 days.

4. Before serving, remove the pie from the freezer and allow it to sit at room temperature for 20–30 minutes.

"Strawberries are the angels of the earth, innocent and sweet with green leafy wings reaching heavenward." – *Jasmine Heiler*

anna getty's easy green organic

sautéed apples with vanilla ice cream

SERVES 6

I came up with this recipe one night when I was craving something sweet. A plain apple wasn't sweet enough, but I didn't want to make anything complicated. This simple, clean-tasting, and delightful dessert is the result. Use whatever apples you have lying around. Organic brandy is easier to come by these days and adds a nice flavor to the apples.

4	Fuji apples, peeled, cored, and cut into ½-inch slices
	Juice of ½ lemon
2	tablespoons unsalted butter
2	teaspoons vanilla extract
1	tablespoon brandy
1	teaspoon ground cinnamon
⅓	cup light brown sugar
	Pinch of salt
3	cups vanilla ice cream
	Handful of coarsely chopped walnuts for garnish

1. In a medium bowl, mix the apples with the lemon juice. (The lemon juice will prevent the apples from turning brown.)

2. In a large sauté pan, melt the butter over medium heat. Add the apples and cook for 10 minutes, stirring occasionally. Add the vanilla, brandy, cinnamon, brown sugar, and salt and cook for another 5 to 6 minutes, until the apples have softened but are still firm. Remove from the heat and set aside.

3. Scoop ½ cup of vanilla ice cream into each of 6 small bowls. Top each scoop with 5 to 6 apple slices and spoon some of the cooking juices over the apples. Garnish with the walnuts.

an apple a day

If you're raising kids, the single most important fruit to buy organically is apples. They are nutritional superstars as long as they are consumed with the peel on, but the average conventional apple contains at least 3 pesticide residues. Peeling the apples eliminates most of the residues, but at far too high a nutritional cost. It reduces the fruit's nutrient levels by one-third to one-half.

Only 2.2 percent of the 743 apple samples tested for pesticide residues in 2005 by the U.S. Department of Agriculture contained none, and most of those samples were probably organic. Twenty-five percent of the samples tested had 5 or more residues and almost 2 percent contained 7 or 8.

Fortunately, most of these residues are either relatively low-risk fungicides or are present in very low levels. Still, apples account for a significant share of total dietary pesticide risk, especially for kids. It is not uncommon for a conventional apple sample to contain two different organophosphate residues, despite the Environmental Protection Agency's efforts over the past 10 years to implement the Food Quality Protection Act.

Both domestically grown and imported conventional apples made the lists of the top ten fruits in terms of their Dietary Risk Index scores, but fortunately, apples land toward the bottom of both lists, with scores of 44 and 30, respectively.

Studies on 3 continents have shown that organic apples taste better and last longer because of the generally higher levels of antioxidants and other natural phytochemicals present.

couscous and currant pudding

SERVES 6

Made from semolina flour, couscous is a staple in Northern African cuisine. While it usually appears in savory dishes, in this recipe it takes center stage as a dessert. I chose currants instead of raisins for their daintiness, but feel free to substitute raisins. The sweetness in this dessert is very subtle, which makes it perfect for people who don't like sugary desserts. It is great paired with Moroccan mint tea.

⅓	cup currants
1	cup couscous
2	cups milk
½	teaspoon ground cinnamon
2	tablespoons granulated sugar
1	tablespoon brown sugar
2	teaspoons vanilla extract
⅛	teaspoon ground cardamom
⅛	teaspoon salt
1	large egg

1. In a small saucepan, bring 1¼ cups water and the currants to a boil. Add the couscous, stirring constantly. Remove from the heat and cover. Let the couscous stand for 5 minutes until the water is absorbed. Fluff with a fork and set aside.

2. In another small saucepan, combine the remaining ingredients and simmer on low heat for 5 minutes, or until the mixture just begins to thicken. Stir in the couscous, making sure to break up any clumps. Cook on low to medium heat, stirring rapidly, for 4 to 5 minutes.

3. Pour the mixture into six 6-ounce ramekins. Cover and refrigerate for 1 hour.

4. Remove from refrigerator and let sit for 10 minutes before serving.

coconut custard with fresh mango and mint chutney

SERVES 6

When I spent time in Thailand, I ate my fair share of coconuts, and fell in love with coconut milk. Creamy coconut milk is so complex, with a rich flavor that makes it a welcome addition to sweet and savory dishes. In this custard, I substitute agar for eggs, gelatin, or milk. Agar is a vegetarian gelatin substitute derived from seaweed. Used throughout Asia in desserts and as a thickener for soups and sauces, it works wonderfully in puddings, cakes, and custards. Like gelatin, it is flavorless. You can find it at large branch health food stores or online.

Two 14-ounce cans coconut milk

²/₃ cup sugar

¼ cup agar

2 small fresh mangoes, cut into ¼-inch cubes

8 fresh mint leaves, cut into thin strips

1 teaspoon fresh lemon juice

1 tablespoon agave nectar

1 teaspoon unsweetened coconut flakes, toasted in a dry pan for 3 to 4 minutes

1. Combine the coconut milk, sugar, and agar in a medium saucepan and bring to a boil.

2. Lower the heat and simmer for about 10 to 15 minutes, or until the agar has dissolved.

3. Pour the hot coconut milk into six 6-ounce pudding cups or ramekins. Let cool to room temperature and then refrigerate for at least 2 hours or overnight.

4. Mix together the mango cubes, mint, lemon juice, agave nectar, and toasted coconut in a small bowl and let macerate for 30 minutes, stirring occasionally.

5. When the custards have set, spoon about 2 tablespoons of the mango chutney onto each custard. I prefer the custards chilled but you can serve them at room temperature as well.

mango bread pudding

I have never been a huge fan of bread pudding, but for some reason this bread pudding takes the cake, no pun intended. It combines just the right elements of sweet, tart, creamy, and crispy. Everyone who tries it becomes a fan.

1. Preheat the oven to 350 degrees F. Butter a 9-by-11-inch ceramic baking dish.

2. In a medium saucepan, combine the butter, milk, cream, sugar, vanilla, cardamom, and ginger and simmer over low heat, stirring occasionally, until the butter melts and the milk is hot. Remove from the heat and set aside to cool slightly for 4 to 5 minutes.

3. In a small bowl, whisk the eggs and then whisk them steadily into the milk mixture. Continue whisking until blended.

4. Combine the mangoes and bread in a large bowl and mix well. Transfer to the baking dish and pour the milk mixture evenly over the top. Make sure all of the bread pieces are soaked with the mixture, and let sit for 5 minutes.

5. Bake for 45 to 50 minutes, until bubbly and brown. Serve warm but not hot, with whipped cream or vanilla ice cream.

4 tablespoons salted butter

2 cups whole milk

½ cup heavy cream

⅓ cup sugar

2 teaspoons vanilla extract

2 teaspoons ground cardamom

1 teaspoon ground ginger

3 large eggs

2 large mangoes, pitted, peeled, and cut into ½-inch cubes, or two 10-ounce bags frozen mangoes, thawed

6 slices country bread, cut into ½-inch cubes (about 6 cups)

Whipped Cream (page 233) or vanilla ice cream for serving

caramelized banana cream pie

Who doesn't enjoy a good banana cream pie every now and then? Even the most discriminating gourmet can be swayed by its creamy texture. In this version I sauté the bananas in butter and sugar and allow them to caramelize a bit before arranging them on the bottom of the pie shell. Using a pudding mix saves a lot of time and potential anguish.

1. Prepare the pudding according to the instructions on the box. Set aside.

2. Whip the cream until stiff peaks form. Cover and refrigerate.

3. Melt the butter in a large sauté pan over medium heat, add the bananas, and stir in the sugar. Sauté the bananas for 5 to 8 minutes, stirring constantly, until the bananas are lightly browned.

4. Spoon the bananas over the bottom of the pie crust, and then pour the vanilla pudding over the fruit. Cover the pudding with the whipped cream. Top with the toasted coconut and chill the pie for at least 2 hours. Serve chilled.

COOK'S NOTE: *Many premade graham cracker crusts on the market are made with hydrogenated oils. Look for premade piecrusts that are natural or organic. Arrowhead Mills makes a great graham cracker crust that is free of hydrogenated oils and is made with mostly organic ingredients.*

1 box vanilla pudding mix or instant vanilla pudding mix

1 cup whipping cream

1 tablespoon unsalted butter

2 ripe bananas, sliced

2 tablespoons sugar

1 Basic Graham Cracker Crust (facing page) or premade graham cracker pie crust

2½ tablespoons finely shredded unsweetened coconut, toasted in a dry pan for 3 to 4 minutes

basic graham cracker crust

1. Preheat the oven to 350 degrees F.

2. Break the graham crackers into pieces small enough to fit into the bowl of a food processor. Turn on the motor and process until crumbs form. Alternatively, put the graham crackers into a sealed bag and use a rolling pin to crush the crackers by rolling over them repeatedly until crumbs form. Transfer the crumbs to a medium bowl. Add the sugar and margarine and mix well.

3. Transfer the mixture to an ungreased 9-inch pie plate and, using your hands, press the mixture firmly into the pie plate so that the crust is about ⅛ inch thick.

4. Bake for 8 to 10 minutes, or until the edges are golden.

18 graham crackers

¼ cup sugar

⅓ cup soy margarine or butter, melted

did you know. . .

The edible part of a banana generally does not contain a significant number of pesticides. Nevertheless, in 2006, about 30 percent of the 742 samples tested contained 2 or more pesticide residues. One oddball sample contained 8 residues! Postharvest fungicides were by far the most commonly detected pesticide—66 percent of 742 samples contained thiabendazole and 31 percent showed traces of imazalil.

dried cranberry and toasted hazelnut macaroons

MAKES 16 TO 18 COOKIES

When I was a child, coconut macaroons were my absolute favorite cookie. With this more grown-up version, I am able to carry my macaroon obsession into adulthood.

2	teaspoons vanilla extract
1½	cups finely shredded unsweetened coconut
½	cup hazelnuts, finely chopped
¼	cup dried cranberries, coarsely chopped
2	large egg whites
	Pinch of salt
⅔	cup sugar

1. Preheat the oven to 325 degrees F. Line two baking sheets with parchment paper and spray them with nonstick cooking spray.

2. In a medium bowl, mix together the vanilla, coconut, hazelnuts, and dried cranberries.

3. In a separate bowl, use a whisk or electric mixer to beat the egg whites with the salt until soft peaks form. Sprinkle 1 teaspoon of the sugar into the egg whites and beat until glossy. Fold in the remaining sugar and then fold in the coconut and hazelnut mixture.

4. Using a tablespoon, drop the batter by the spoonful, 1 inch apart, onto the baking sheets.

5. Bake for 15 to 20 minutes, or until golden. Allow the macaroons to cool on the baking sheets for 5 minutes and then transfer them to wire racks to cool completely.

did you know. . .

Convection ovens cook food 25 percent faster than conventional ovens. They use a fan to rapidly drive heat from the source to the food.

zucchini and sweet potato bread with pumpkin seeds and dried cherries

MAKES ONE 9-BY-5-INCH LOAF

This is my favorite bread recipe, period. It's really an anytime sweet: in the morning for breakfast, slathered with butter; as an afternoon snack with a cup of tea; or after dinner as a dessert. This richly textured bread has so many layers. The crumble topping, the crunchiness of the pumpkin seeds, and the tartness of the dried cherries add a lot of color and texture to this yummy bread, which I make with a garnet yam instead of an actual sweet potato. Make a double batch because it won't last long on the kitchen counter. And did I mention it is packed with nutrition, even though my daughter calls it cake?

1. Preheat the oven to 350 degrees F. Butter a 9-by-5-by-3-inch loaf pan.

2. To make the topping, mix together the flour, brown sugar, and pumpkin seeds. Cut in the butter with a pastry cutter until the mixture resembles coarse meal. Set aside.

3. To make the bread, in a medium bowl, sift together the flour, baking powder, baking soda, salt, and cinnamon.

4. In a large bowl, beat together the sugar, oil, eggs, and vanilla. Mix in the zucchini and yam. Add the flour mixture, pumpkin seeds, and dried cherries and stir well. Transfer the batter to the prepared loaf pan. Sprinkle the topping evenly over the batter.

5. Bake the bread for 1½ hours, or until a toothpick inserted into the middle of the bread comes out clean.

6. Let the zucchini bread cool in the pan before removing it from the pan to serve.

crumble topping

- ¼ cup unbleached all-purpose flour
- 3 tablespoons brown sugar
- 1 tablespoon pumpkin seeds
- 2 tablespoons cold unsalted butter, cut into small pieces

zucchini and sweet potato bread

- 2 cups unbleached all-purpose flour
- ¼ teaspoon aluminum-free baking powder
- 1 teaspoon baking soda
- ½ teaspoon salt
- 2 teaspoons ground cinnamon
- 1 cup sugar
- 1 cup vegetable oil
- 3 large eggs
- 2 teaspoons vanilla extract
- 1 cup grated zucchini (about 1½ small zucchini)
- 1 cup grated garnet yam (about ½ large garnet yam)
- ¾ cup pumpkin seeds
- ¾ cup dried cherries

juliet's no-fail banana bread with dark chocolate chips

MAKES ONE 9-BY-5-INCH LOAF

I had long been searching for the perfect banana bread recipe when my dear friend Juliet Angus shared her version with me. It must be the soy margarine, buttermilk, and crunchy walnut topping that make this recipe stand out from all the rest. I threw in dark chocolate chips for chocolate lovers. You could also cut up a dark chocolate bar into rough, choppy bits instead of using chocolate chips; it makes the bread slices look a little more fancy.

2	cups unbleached all-purpose flour
1	teaspoon salt
1	teaspoon baking soda
1½	cups sugar
½	cup (1 stick) soy margarine, melted
2	teaspoons vanilla extract
¼	cup buttermilk
2	large eggs, beaten
3	very ripe bananas, mashed (about 1½ cups)
½	cup dark chocolate chips
½	cup coarsely chopped walnuts

walnut topping

¼	cup ground walnuts
1	tablespoon light brown sugar

1. Preheat the oven to 350 degrees F. Grease a 9-by-5-inch loaf pan.

2. In a medium bowl, sift together the flour, salt, and baking soda.

3. In a large bowl, cream together the sugar and margarine with a wooden spoon or an electric mixer. Stir in the vanilla and buttermilk. Add the eggs and bananas and mix well. Add the sifted ingredients, stirring until just combined. Fold in the chocolate chips and walnuts. Pour the batter into the loaf pan.

4. To make the topping, mix together the ground walnuts and brown sugar and sprinkle the mixture over the batter.

5. Bake for 1 hour and 15 minutes, or until the top of the bread is brown and a toothpick inserted in the middle of the loaf comes out clean.

6. Let the banana bread cool in the pan before serving.

amy b.'s espresso chocolate pudding cake

SERVES 6

Once I completed the recipes for this book, I realized that I had not included a chocolate dessert (other than the chocolate-dipped trio on page 231). As a devoted chocolate lover, I was taken aback by the omission. Coincidentally, my chef friend and amazing recipe tester Amy Brown had just finished developing a chocolate pudding cake recipe for a contest. She brought one of these little cakes over for me to taste, and I literally fell to my knees begging her for the recipe. She obliged, and I am thrilled to include it. These little pudding cakes are sent directly from heaven—there's no better dessert for a true chocoholic. Look for the brioche at your local bakery.

6 ounces bittersweet chocolate

2 cups heavy cream

½ cup plus 2 tablespoons cane sugar

4 large egg yolks

¼ cup brewed espresso

3 cups brioche bread crumbs (about 3 small loaves brioche; see Cook's Note)

Whipped Cream for serving (page 233)

Thinly sliced fresh mint for garnish (optional)

Edible flower petals for garnish (optional; see page 129)

1. Preheat the oven to 350 degrees F. Grease six 5-ounce ramekins with butter.

2. Melt the chocolate in a double boiler or a nonreactive heat-proof bowl placed over a pot of simmering water. Remove from the heat and let cool slightly.

3. In a small saucepan, heat the cream and sugar over medium heat until the sugar is dissolved, stirring occasionally. Make sure the cream mixture does not bubble over.

4. In a large bowl, lightly whisk the egg yolks. Slowly add the warm cream mixture to the eggs, stirring briskly to prevent the egg yolks from curdling. Add the melted chocolate slowly, whisking constantly until the mixture is well blended. Add the espresso, stirring until well combined.

5. Add the bread crumbs to the chocolate mixture and use your hands to fully incorporate them, making sure to break up any lumps. Let the batter sit for 2 minutes.

6. Spoon the batter into the ramekins and put them in a 9-by-13-inch baking dish, spacing them about ½ inch apart. Slowly pour 2½ cups of warm water into the baking dish, or enough to come halfway up the ramekins, to create a *bain-marie*, or water bath. This will help the pudding cakes bake evenly.

(continued on next page)

7. Cover the baking dish with recycled foil or with a small baking tray and bake the cakes until set, 25 to 30 minutes. (When completely baked, the tops of the pudding cakes will no longer jiggle.)

8. Remove from the oven, uncover the ramekins, and allow the cakes to sit in the water bath for 5 minutes. Serve the cakes in the ramekins, or run a butter knife around the inside of each ramekin and invert it onto a small dessert plate. Serve with Whipped Cream (page 233) and garnish with the mint or edible flower petals, if desired.

COOK'S NOTE: *To make brioche bread crumbs, cut the brioche loaves into hunks, put in the bowl of a food processor, and pulse until you have smooth, even crumbs. If you can't find brioche bread, substitute freshly baked egg bread or a croissant—they are similar in texture.*

green tip

Be careful when choosing chocolate. Cacao beans are imported into the United States from developing countries where, for the most part, both humans and the environment are being exploited. Be sure to look for chocolate labeled "fair-trade certified." Companies that place fair trade labels on their products guarantee that the workers receive fair wages for their work. (The same goes for coffee.)

death by chocolate

"Twill make Old Women Young and Fresh;
Create New Motions of the Flesh. And cause
them long for you know what, If they but
taste of chocolate."
—*James Wadworth,*
A History of the Nature and Quality of Chocolate

I live and breathe chocolate. I snack on chocolate bars, make cups of creamy hot chocolate, throw cocoa powder into fruit shakes, and devour chocolate desserts at every opportunity. If I could somehow wear it, I would. It makes no difference what type of chocolate it is—dark, milk, white—I love it all.

The good news is that recent health studies have done nothing but praise chocolate. Research has shown that the flavonoids in dark chocolate fight free radicals, which are highly reactive molecules that can cause brain and tissue damage, as well as lower blood pressure and cholesterol levels. Chocolate contains nearly eight times more antioxidants than strawberries according to nutritionist Sofia Segounis. The darker the chocolate, the more antioxidants it contains. In addition, dark chocolate contains serotonin, which acts as an antidepressant—no wonder eating chocolate makes us so happy. With so many health benefits, chocolate lovers should indulge guilt free.

Certified organic chocolate is a relatively new category. As an organic food, no ingredient in the chocolate may be genetically modified. In addition, if milk is used in the chocolate, it must not contain rBGH, a growth hormone given to cows to increase milk production. The cacao bean itself must come from organically grown plots. (According to the Pesticide Awareness Network, conventional cocoa is number two after cotton in terms of pesticide use.) Organic chocolate, free of any artificial ingredients, is thought to maximize the health benefits present in the cacao bean.

There's also an environmental aspect to organic chocolate. Cacao trees grow in rain forests, and many producers are working to ensure that no rain forest land is destroyed to harvest the beans. Many organic chocolate producers also work with farmers to establish sustainable farming practices and have fair-trade policies.

dark chocolate–dipped trio:
strawberries, black olives, and walnuts

SERVES 6 TO 12

This dessert is for the sophisticated palate, with a contrast of sweet and savory. It can be served as a light dessert or with coffee after the main dessert.

One 3½-ounce bar dark chocolate

12 strawberries, with stems on

1 teaspoon red peppercorns, crushed with a mortar and pestle or peppermill

12 walnut halves

½ teaspoon pink Himalayan salt or another flaky gourmet salt

12 Moroccan olives with pits

1. Line a baking sheet or serving tray with parchment paper.

2. Melt the chocolate in a double boiler or in a nonreactive heat-proof bowl over a pot of simmering water. When the chocolate is completely melted, stir thoroughly.

3. Holding onto the hull of the strawberry, dip each one into the melted chocolate and place it on the baking sheet. Sprinkle crushed red peppercorns on top.

4. Drop the walnut pieces into the chocolate and stir until coated with chocolate. With a slotted spoon, transfer the walnuts to the baking sheet and sprinkle them with the salt.

5. Put the olives in the chocolate and stir until coated. (It's important to do the olives last because they tend to be salty.) Transfer them to the baking sheet with a slotted spoon. (There will most likely be chocolate left over in the double boiler or bowl. Add milk, a pinch of cayenne, and about a tablespoon of sugar to the melted chocolate to make Mexican hot chocolate—if you dare.)

6. Place the baking sheet in the refrigerator and let the berries, nuts, and olives set for at least 1 hour. Remove from the refrigerator at least 15 minutes before serving.

whipped cream

Many of the recipes in this chapter taste great with a dollop of whipped cream. I adore freshly whipped cream, but whipping cream by hand isn't necessarily easy for everyone. Here is a no-fail way to get beautiful stiff peaks of whipped cream.

1	cup cold whipping cream
½	teaspoon vanilla extract
1	tablespoon sugar

Put a medium glass, ceramic, copper, or a stainless-steel bowl in the freezer for 10 minutes. Remove the bowl from the freezer and add the whipping cream, vanilla, and sugar. Using a whisk, beat the cream rapidly for 2½ to 3 minutes. You can use a hand mixer, which will make the process go much more quickly, but a whisk is the greener choice, and your guests will truly appreciate hand-whipped cream. For variety, in place of the vanilla add almond or mint extract to the cream before whipping, or even maple syrup. Play around and add whatever flavors you like.

menu suggestions

LA DOLCE VITA—AN EASY ITALIAN DINNER

Real Deal Bruschetta

Fusilli with Toasted Walnuts, Olives, Capers, Toasted Bread Crumbs,
and Pecorino

Balsamic-Broiled Asparagus with Shaved Parmesan Cheese

Berries with Basil and Lavender-Honey Yogurt Drizzle

IT'S FINALLY SPRING SUNDAY BRUNCH

Arugula and Strawberry Salad with Pumpkin Seeds and Lemon Vinaigrette

Warm Potato Salad with Lentils and Capers

Pea Tendril and Goat Cheese Frittata

Zucchini and Sweet Potato Bread with Pumpkin Seeds and Dried Cherries

A SIMPLE MEDITERRANEAN MEAL

Saffron Cauliflower Soup

Steamed Halibut with Greek Salad Salsa

Summer Zucchini Salad with Pine Nuts and Parmesan

Couscous and Currant Pudding

VEGETARIAN'S DELIGHT DINNER

Quinoa Croquettes with Cilantro Yogurt Sauce

Creamy Butternut Squash and Macadamia Nut Soup with Roasted Poblano
Chile Cream

Baked Portobello Mushrooms with Avocado and Pesto

Carrot Caraway Salad

Sautéed Apples with Vanilla Ice Cream

A HAPPY HOLIDAY DINNER

Bacon and Sage Leaf–Wrapped Scallops

Winter Chestnut Apple Soup

Garden Herb and Garlic Clay Pot Chicken

Maple-Orange Glazed Carrots

Figs in Port Wine with Greek Yogurt

DATE NIGHT
Wild Mushroom Soup with Peas and Sweet Potatoes
Seared Bay Scallops with Orzo and Sun-Dried Tomato Cream Sauce
Sautéed Baby Squash with Tarragon and Soy Sauce
Amy B.'s Espresso Chocolate Pudding Cake

MAKE-AHEAD FAMILY MEAL
Super Easy Black Bean and Turkey Chili
Wild Rice and Chicken Waldorf Salad
Caramelized Banana Cream Pie

FRIDAY NIGHT DINNER PARTY
Fennel Soup
Paul's Filet Mignon with Whiskey Cream Sauce
Sage Skillet Potatoes
Roasted Baby Beets with Horseradish Cream and Walnuts
Mini–Strawberry Rhubarb Crumbles

A SIMPLE THAI SUPPER
Thai Fish Medallions with Cucumber Relish
Glass Noodle Stir-Fry
Thai Carrot Salad with Toasted Almonds
Coconut Custard with Fresh Mango and Mint Chutney

ASIAN INSPIRATION
Pan-Fried Sake Shrimp
Hearty Miso Soup
Warm Asian Mushroom Salad
Cold Sesame Soba Noodle Salad

A DINNER TO IMPRESS YOUR FRIENDS

Fried Polenta with Sautéed Wild Mushrooms and Chipotle Cream Sauce

Ginger Risotto

Beet and Watercress Salad with Walnuts and Curry Vinaigrette

Dark Chocolate–Dipped Trio: Strawberries, Black Olives, and Walnuts

A LATE SUMMER SUPPER

Roasted Tomato and Goat Cheese Toasts

Barbecue Baked Alaskan Salmon

Sautéed Fresh Corn with Cilantro and Scallions

Pear and Blueberry Crisp with Brown Sugar Sour Cream Topping

ITALIAN-WITH-A-TWIST LUNCHEON

White Bean and Tuna Salad with Fresh Mozzarella, Red Onion,
and Balsamic Vinaigrette

Pasta Fresca

John Pepper's Exotic Green Beans

Dried Cranberry and Toasted Hazelnut Macaroons

MIXING IT UP DINNER

Red Quinoa Salad

Double Lemon Chicken Breasts with Fresh Tomato Basil Salsa

Sautéed Swiss Chard with Garlic, Raisins, and Pine Nuts

Dates Stuffed Two Ways

A GREAT ANYTIME DINNER

Pan-Fried Tofu Squares with Sweet Chile Sauce

Coconut Chicken Curry over Basmati Rice with Almonds and Raisins

Garlicky Baby Bok Choy

Mango Bread Pudding

organic california wines

Below is a list of organic California wines to get you started and some information about organic and biodynamic wines. For more information about organic wines, visit the Organic Wine Journal at www. organicwinejournal.com. I have noted when a wine is made with organic grapes certified by the California Certified Organic Farmers (CCOF), and when they have been grown biodynamically. Biodynamic farming goes beyond organic, treating the farm as part of a larger ecosystem. This approach incorporates chemical-free solutions to things such as pests and weeds and takes astronomical considerations into account during planting. The information for this list comes from the Town Hall Coalition (www.townhall coalition.org/resources).

Barra of Mendocino and Redwood Valley Vineyards

7051 N. State St., Redwood Valley, CA 95470

T: 707-485-8771 F: 707-485-0147

Web: www.barraofmendocino.com

E-mail: info@barraofmendocino.com

Wines made with CCOF-certified organically grown grapes. Whites: Chardonnay, Muscat Canelli. Reds: Sangioviese, Pinot Noir, Petite Sirah, Zinfandel, Cabernet Sauvignon

Benziger Family Winery and Vineyard

1883 London Ranch Road, Glen Ellen, CA 95442

T: 888-490-2739 F: 707-935-3016

Web: www.benziger.com E-mail: greatwine@benziger.com

CCOF-certified and biodynamically grown grapes. Whites: Sauvignon Blanc, Chardonnay. Reds: Tribute, Estate Zinfandel, Sonoma Mountain Red (McNab Vineyard)

Bonterra Vineyards

2231 McNab Ranch Road, Ukiah, CA 95482

T: 800-846-8637, 707-744-1250 F: 707-570-0398

Web: www.bonterra.com E-mail: bonterra@bonterra.com

Wines made with CCOF-certified organically grown grapes. Whites: Chardonnay, Sauvignon Blanc, Viognier, Muscat. Reds: Cabernet Sauvignon, Merlot, Syrah, Zinfandel

Buchlin Old Hill Ranch Winery

8 Old Hill Ranch Road, Glen Ellen, CA 95442

T: 707-933-1726 F: 707-938-9169

Web: www.buckzin.com E-mail: kin@buckzin.com

Wines made with certified organic grapes. Reds: Old Hill Ranch Zinfandel, Cabernet Sauvignon. White: Compagni Portis Vineyard Gewürtztraminer

Coturri Winery and Vineyard

6725 Enterprise Road, Glen Ellen, CA 95442

T: 707-525-9126 F: 707-542-8039

Web: www.coturriwinery.com E-mail: tony@coturriwinery.com

CCOF-certified estate wines. Reds: Cabernet Sauvignon, Cabernet Blend, Sangiovese, Zinfandel, Merlot, Pinot Noir, Syrah, Albarello, Côte des Cailloux

Davis Bynum Winery

8075 Westside Road, Healdsburg, CA 95448

T: 866-442-7547 F: 707-433-0939

Web: www.davisbynum.com E-mail: celeste@davisbynum.com

Estate-grown grapes and wines are CCOF-certified organic. White: Chardonnay. Red: Pinot Noir

Deerfield Ranch Winery

1310 Warm Springs Road, Glen Ellen, CA 95442

T: 707-833-5215 F: 707-833-1312

Web: www.deerfieldranch.com

E-mail: winery@deerfieldranch.com

Wines made with CCOF-certified organically grown grapes. Reds: Red Rex, Super T Rex, DRX Meritage, Merlot Cuvee

Del Bondio Wine Company

1315 Bella Oaks Lane, Napa, CA 94558

T: 888-223-DELB (3352) F: 707-963-2129

Web: www.delbondio.com E-mail: delbondio@comcast.net

Wines made with CCOF-certified organically grown grapes. Reds: Cabernet Sauvignon, Syrah. White: Chardonnay

Frey Vineyards and Winery

14000 Tomki Road, Redwood Valley, CA 95470

T: 800-760-3739, 707-485-5177 F: 707-485-7875

Web: www.freywine.com E-mail: info@freywine.com

Wines made with CCOF-certified organically grown grapes. (Estate wines are Demeter-certified and biodynamic.) Whites: Gewürtztraminer, Chardonnay, Natural White, Sauvignon Blanc. Reds: Natural Red, Zinfandel, Pinot Noir, Petite Sirah, Sangiovese, Merlot, Cabernet Sauvignon, Syrah, Late Harvest Zinfandel. Wines made with biodynamic grapes: Whites—Chardonnay, Sauvignon Blanc; reds—Merlot, Cabernet Sauvignon, Petite Sirah, Zinfandel, Syrah

Frog's Leap Winery and Vineyard

8815 Conn Creek Road, Rutherford, CA 94573

T: 800-959-4704, 707-963-4704 F: 707-963-0242

Web: www.frogsleap.com E-mail: ribbit@frogsleap.com

All estate-grown grapes are CCOF-certified organic. Reds: Zinfandel, Merlot, Cabernet Sauvignon, Petite Sirah, Rutherford (Cabernet), Pink (Rosé). Whites: Sauvignon Blanc, Chardonnay, Frögenbeerenauslese

Graziano Family of Wines

13251 S. Highway 101, Suite 3, Hopland, CA 95449

T: 707-744-VINO (8466) F: 707-744-8470

Web: www.grazianofamilyofwines.com

E-mail: info@grazianofamilyofwines.com

Wines made with certified organically grown grapes. Red: Redwood Valley Zinfandel (Robert Parker Vineyard)

Grgich Hills Estate

PO Box 450, 1829 St. Helena Highway, Rutherford, CA 94573

T: 800-532-3057 F: 707-963-8725

Web: www.grgich.com E-mail: info@grgich.com

Grapes are organically and biodynamically farmed. Reds: Cabernet Sauvignon, Zinfandel, Merlot. Whites: Fumé Blanc, Violetta (Napa Valley blend), Chardonnay

Kaz Vineyard & Winery

215 Adobe Canyon Road, Kenwood, CA 95452

T: 877-833-2536 F: 707-833-1244

Web: www.kazwinery.com E-mail: kaz@vom.com

Wines made organically with organically grown grapes. Reds: Kazorouge (blend), Barbera, Cabernet Sauvignon, Merlot, Red Said Fred (blend), Mary Tauge (Cabernet Sauvignon, Petit Verdot), Mourvedre. Ports: White Port, Blush Port, Red Port. White: Chardonnay

Le Vin Estate Winery & Vineyards

PO Box 473, Cloverdale, CA 95425

T: 707-894-2304 F: 707-894-1080

Web: www.levinwinery.com E-mail: hrh@sonic.net

Wines made from organically grown grapes. Reds: Merlot, Cabernet Sauvignon, Syrah, Pinot Noir

Lolonis Winery and Vineyard

1905 Road D, Redwood Valley, CA 95470

T: 925-938-8066 F: 925-938-8069

Web: www.lolonis.com

Wines made with CCOF-certified organically grown grapes. Reds: Cuvee V Ladybug Red, Zinfandel, Merlot, Cabernet Sauvignon, Syrah, Petite Sirah—Sisters Blend, Petros (blend). Whites: Ladybug White Old Vines Cuvee II, Antigone (Late Harvest Chardonnay), Eugenia Sauvignon Blanc

Madonna Estate

5400 Old Sonoma Road, Napa, CA 94559

T: 707-255-8864 F: 707-257-2778

Web: www.madonnaestate.com

E-mail: mail@madonnaestate.com

Made with CCOF-certified organically grown grapes. Reds: Pinot Noir, Merlot, Cabernet Sauvignon, Dolcetto, Due Regazze Pinot Noir Riserva. Whites: Chardonnay, Muscat Canelli, Gewürztraminer, Pinot Grigio, Riesling

Mason Cellars Winery

714 First Street, Napa, CA 94559

T: 707-255-0658 F: 707-255-0656

Web: www.masoncellars.com E-mail: megan@masoncellars.com

Made with organically grown grapes. White: Sauvignon Blanc. Reds: Merlot, Cabernet Sauvignon

Masút

PO Box 348, Redwood Valley, CA 95470

T: 707-485-5466 F: 707-485-9664

Web: www.masut.com E-mail: jacobfetzer@masut.com

Made from organic and biodynamic grapes. Reds: Pinot Noir, Sangiovese

Moon Mountain Vineyard

1700 Moon Mountain Drive, Sonoma, CA 95476

T: 707-996-5870

Web: www.moonmountainvineyard.com

E-mail: MMNinfo@moonmountainvineyard.com

Wines made from organically grown grapes. Whites: Chardonnay, Sauvignon Blanc. Reds: Cabernet Franc, Cabernet Sauvignon, Merlot, Syrah, Zinfandel, Petit Verdot. Port: Zinfandel

Napa Wine Company Vineyard and Winery

7830-40 St. Helena Highway, Oakville, CA 94562

T: 707-944-8669 F: 707-944-9749

Web: www.napawineco.com

E-mail: moreinfo@napawineco.com

Wines made with CCOF-certified organically grown grapes. Whites: Sauvignon Blanc, Pinot Blanc. Reds: Cabernet Sauvignon, Zinfandel, Pinot Noir, Petite Sirah

Parducci Signature Mendocino Wine Company

501 Parducci Road, Ukiah, CA 95482

T: 707-463-5350

Web: www.mendocinowineco.com

E-mail: info@mendocinowineco.com

Wines made from organic grapes. Whites: Pinot Grigio, Sauvignon Blanc, Chardonnay, Muscato. Reds: Petite Sirah, Zinfandel, Pinot Noir

Porter Creek Vineyards

8735 Westside Road, Healdsburg, CA 95448

T: 707-433-6321 F: 707-433-4245

Web: www.portercreekvineyards.com

E-mail: info@portercreekvineyards.com

Grapes are organically certified and biodynamically grown. Whites: Chardonnay, Viognier. Reds: Pinot Noir, Syrah, Carignane

Quivira Vineyards

4900 W. Dry Creek Road, Healdsburg, CA 95448

T: 800-292-8339, 707-431-8333 F: 707-431-1664

Web: www.quivirawine.com E-mail: quivira@quivirawine.com

Certified organic grapes and biodynamic certification. Whites: Sauvignon Blanc, Steelhead Sauvignon Blanc, Grenache Rosé. Reds: Steelhead Zinfandel, Zinfandel, Grenache, Syrah

Robert Sinskey Vineyards

6320 Silverado Trail, Napa, CA 94558

T: 800-869-2030, 707-944-9090

Web: www.robertsinskey.com E-mail: rsv@robertsinskey.com

Wines are made from organic and biodynamic grapes. Whites: Abraxas, Pinot Gris. Reds: Cabernet Sauvignon RSV, RSV Proprietary Blend, Merlot, Pinot Noir

Rubicon Estate

1991 St. Helena Highway, Rutherford, CA 94573

T: 800-782-4266

Web: www.rubiconestate.com E-mail: info@rubiconestate.com

Estate wines made with CCOF-certified organic grapes. White: Blancaneaux (blend). Reds: Rubicon (blend), RC Reserve Syrah, Merlot, Cabernet Franc, CASK Cabernet, Edizione Pennino Zinfandel

Sky Saddle Wines

5241 Old Redwood Highway Suite G, Santa Rosa, CA 95403

T: 707-483-6645 F: 866-224-0051

Web: www.skysaddle.com E-mail: skysaddle@earthlink.net

Wines made with organic and/or biodynamic grapes. Reds: Cabernet Sauvignon, Zinfandel, Syrah, Pinot Noir, Sangiovese. White: Chardonnay

Spottswoode Estate Vineyard & Winery

1902 Madrona Avenue, St. Helena, CA 94574

T: 707-963-0134 F: 707-963-2886

Web: www.spottswoode.com E-mail: estate@spottswoode.com

Wines made with CCOF-certified organically grown grapes. Red: Cabernet Sauvignon. White: Sauvignon Blanc

**Torres Family Vineyards
Marimar Estate**

11400 Graton Road, Sebastopol, CA 95472

T: 707-823-4365, ext. 101 F: 707-823-4496

Web: www.marimarestate.com

E-mail: info@marimarestate.com

Estates wines made from organically grown grapes. White: Chardonnay. Reds: Pinot Noir, Syrah-Tempranillo

Volker Eisele Family Estate Vineyard and Winery

3080 Lower Chiles Valley Road, St. Helena, CA 94574

T: 707-965-9485

Web: www.volkereiselefamilyestate.com

E-mail: info@volkereiselefamilyestate.com

Wines made with CCOF-certified organically grown grapes. White: Gemini (blend). Reds: Cabernet Sauvignon, Terzetto (blend)

Wild Hog Vineyard

PO Box 189, Cazadero, CA 95421

T: 707-847-3687

Web: www.wildhogvineyard.com

E-mail: info@wildhogwineyard.com

Wines made with CCOF-certified organically grown grapes. Reds: Zinfandel, Pinot Noir

Yorkville Cellars

25701 Highway 128, Yorkville, CA 95494

T: 707-894-9177 F: 707-894-2426

Web: www.yorkville-cellars.com E-mail: yvcellars@pacific.net

Estate Wines made from CCOF-certified organic grapes. Whites: Sauvignon Blanc, Semillon, Eleanor of Aquitaine (blend). Reds: Merlot, Richard the Lion-Heart (blend), Malbec, Cabernet Sauvignon, Petit Verdot, Cabernet Franc

resources

Here is a list of the organizations and companies that I turn to when making my green and organic choices, and when searching for reliable information. I hope this list helps you find your way.

EDUCATION

Earth 911

www.earth911.org

An online resource to help you recycle and give you solutions for being more green.

Environmental Defense Fund

www.edf.org

Creating lasting solutions to the most serious environmental problems.

Environmental Working Group

www.ewg.org

A team of scientists, engineers, policy experts, lawyers, and computer programmers who pore over legal documents, scientific data, and their own laboratory tests to expose threats to the environment and our health. Their Food News (www.foodnews. org) provides a list of forty-three fruits and vegetables ranked according to their measured levels of pesticides. They also have a downloadable list of the "Dirty Dozen," the twelve conventionally grown fruits and veggies to avoid because of their high levels of pesticide residues.

Healthy Child Healthy World

www.healthychild.org

Dedicated to protecting the health and well-being of children from harmful environmental exposures. An excellent resource for anyone who wants to get toxic chemicals out of their home.

Monterey Bay Aquarium

www.mbayaq.org

Their Seafood Watch Program offers current lists of the United States' most sustainable fish.

The O'Mama Report

www.theorganicreport.com

Organic information and inspiration brought to you by the Organic Trade Association.

The Organic Center

www.organiccenter.org

Generating peer-reviewed scientific information and communicating the verifiable benefits of organic farming and products.

Organic Consumers Association

www.organicconsumers.org

An online and grassroots public interest organization campaigning for health, justice, and sustainability. Focused on promoting the interest of the organic consumer.

Organic Farming Research Foundation

www.ofrf.org

An organization whose mission is to foster the improvement and widespread adoption of organic farming practices.

Slow Food USA

www.slowfoodusa.org

A global, grassroots movement envisioning a world in which all people can eat delicious food that is good for them, good for those who grow it, and good for the planet.

TransFair USA

www.transfairusa.org

A nonprofit organization that audits transactions between U.S. companies offering Fair Trade Certified products and their international suppliers to guarantee the farmers and farm workers were paid a fair, above market price.

KITCHEN AND GARDENING

The AeroGarden

www.aerogrow.com

The AeroGarden grows herbs and vegetables in your kitchen year-round. This a great product for urban apartment dwellers who lack gardening space.

EcoChoices-EcoKitchen

www.ecokitchen.com

Products for the practical, high-quality, natural, and energy efficient kitchen.

Goods for the Garden

www.goodsforthegarden.com

Environmentally friendly garden tools, furniture, pottery and accessories.

Greenfeet

www.greenfeet.com

This online store has trademarked the name "The Planet's Homestore," and for good reason—all of their products are environmentally sound. They have an extensive list of kitchen supplies, from cookware and kitchen textiles to food storage containers.

LifeWithoutPlastic.com

www.lifewithoutplastic.com

A Web site offering non-plastic products, including food storage containers, water bottles, and child and baby products.

Preserve

www.recycline.com

Offers the complete line of recyclable Preserve products, made from 100 percent recycled #5 plastic and from 100 percent postconsumer recycled paper. Their line of products includes cutting boards, storage containers, colanders, cutlery, plates, and tumblers.

Recycle My Old Fridge

www.recyclemyoldfridge.com

For a complete program on your old refrigerator.

ReusableBags.com

www.reusablebags.com

Eco-friendly reusable bags and storage containers, plus facts and news on the plastic bag issue.

Seventh Genaration

www.seventhgeneration.com

One of my favorite companies for home cleaning supplies. They offer a full range of kitchen, bathroom, and home cleaning supplies that are nontoxic. Seventh Generation is an environmentally responsibly run company and is constantly striving to improve their products, which are widely available in supermarkets as well as online.

Shaklee

www.shaklee.com

The company's complete line of Get Clean home cleaning products are safe for the environment. You order the plastic containers only once, and after that they send refills in bags—genius.

VivaTerra

www.vivaterra.com

This home lifestyle Web site offers products that are fair trade, organic, sustainable, and both earth- and people-friendly. It's a one-stop shopping site for stylish accents for your home and garden.

ORGANIC, NATURAL, AND FAIR TRADE FOOD

David Wolfe's Sunfood Nutrition

www.sunfood.com

Offers premium raw organic products, including oils, honeys, olives, nuts, and seeds.

Diamond Organics

www.diamondorganics.com

Since 1990, Diamond Organics has been one of the nation's best sources for farm-fresh, all-organic food, with guaranteed nationwide overnight home delivery, fresh from the California coast. They have a large selection of fresh organic meats.

Eden Organic

www.edenfoods.com

One of the United States' largest organic food producers and suppliers. Their exceptional products include olive oils, quinoa, dried fruits and nuts, misos, and ume plum vinegar.

GoBio!

www.gobiofood.com

Organic specialty items like instant pudding, gelatin, salt, and bouillon.

Living Harvest

www.livingharvest.com

100 percent organic hemp products, including hemp seeds, milk, and oil.

Miyako Oriental Foods

www.coldmountainmiso.com

Offering non-GMO, kosher, and organic soybean miso paste.

Purely Organic

www.purelyorganic.com

The exclusive importer of fine organic Italian products, including pasta, oils, sun-dried tomatoes, olives, and capers.

Shop Organic

www.shoporganic.com

An online store for all things organic, from groceries to personal care items and everything in between. Great bulk buying section.

Starwest Botanicals

www.starwest-botanicals.com

Your online source for more than 3,000 natural products, including the finest in bulk certified organic and kosher herbs and spices, and organic essential oils.

Transition Nutrition

www.royalhimalayan.com

Offers premium raw food ingredients, including Himalayan salt, nuts, agave nectar, raw cacao, and vanilla beans.

Tsar Nicoulai

www.tsarnicoulai.com

Purveyors of sustainable caviar.

OTHER FUN AND HELPFUL WEB SITES FOR THE GREEN AND ORGANIC LIFE

BioBag

www.biobagusa.com

BioBag is the world's largest brand of 100 percent biodegradable and compostable trash bags made from non-GMO corn.

Compost Guide

www.compostguide.com

A complete guide to composting, a blog, and an online store.

Ecofabulous

www.ecofabulous.com

Zem Joaquin is the mistress of all things green. She covers all aspects of lifestyle.

Energy Star

www.energystar.gov

A joint program of the U.S Environmental Protection Agency and the U.S. Department of Energy that helps us all save money and protect the environment by certifying energy-efficient products.

The Lazy Environmenalist

www.lazyenvironmentalist.com

Josh Dorfman reveals easy, stylish, and superconvenient ways to green your lifestyle on this informative site. No guilt trips or sacrifice.

LocalHarvest

www.localharvest.org

LocalHarvest's Web site helps consumers find farmers' markets, family farms, and other sources of sustainably grown food in their area.

Pristine Planet

www.pristineplanet.com

An eco-friendly comparison shopping resource.

Sprig

www.sprig.com

A super-fun Web site. The ultimate in green food, fashion, beauty, home, and lifestyle.

The Sustainable Table's Eat Well Guide

www.eatwellguide.org

The Sustainable Table's Eat Well Guide makes it simple to find sustainable food sources. Just type in your zip code to find sources within a twenty-mile radius.

SELECTED BIBLIOGRAPHY

Berthold-Bond, Annie. *The Green Kitchen Handbook.* New York: HarperPerennial, 1997.

Cox, Jeff. *The Organic Cook's Bible: How to Select and Cook the Best Ingredients on the Market.* Hoboken, NJ: John Wiley and Sons, 2006.

Greene, Alan, M.D. *Raising Baby Green: The Earth Friendly Guide to Pregnancy, Childbirth and Baby Care.* San Francisco: Jossey-Bass, 2007.

Loux, Renee. *The Balanced Plate: The Essential Elements of Whole Foods and Good Health.* New York: Rodale, 2006.

Meyerowitz, Steve. *The Organic Food Guide: How to Shop Smarter and Eat Healthier.* Guilford, CT: The Globe Pequot Press, 2004.

Perry, Luddene and Dan Schultz. *A Field Guide to Buying Organic.* New York: Bantam Dell, 2005.

Rogers, Elizabeth and Kostigen, Thomas M. *The Green Book: The Everyday Guide to Saving The Planet One Simple Step at a Time.* New York: Three Rivers Press, 2007.

The Organic Center for Education. *Core Truths: Serving up the Science Behind Organic Agriculture.* Boulder, CO: 2006.

Toussaint-Samat, Maguelonne. *History of Food.* Paris: Bordas, 1987.

Walters, Charles. *Eco-Farm: An Acres U.S.A. Primer.* Austin, TX: Acres U.S.A., 2003.

index

table of equivalents

The exact equivalents in the following tables have been rounded for convenience.

LIQUID/DRY MEASUREMENTS

U.S.	METRIC
¼ teaspoon	1.25 milliliters
½ teaspoon	2.5 milliliters
1 teaspoon	5 milliliters
1 tablespoon (3 teaspoons)	15 milliliters
1 fluid ounce (2 tablespoons)	30 milliliters
¼ cup	60 milliliters
⅓ cup	80 milliliters
½ cup	120 milliliters
1 cup	240 milliliters
1 pint (2 cups)	480 milliliters
1 quart (4 cups, 32 ounces)	960 milliliters
1 gallon (4 quarts)	3.84 liters
1 ounce (by weight)	28 grams
1 pound	448 grams
2.2 pounds	1 kilogram

LENGTHS

U.S.	METRIC
⅛ inch	3 millimeters
¼ inch	6 millimeters
½ inch	12 millimeters
1 inch	2.5 centimeters

OVEN TEMPERATURES

FAHRENHEIT	CELSIUS	GAS	FAHRENHEIT	CELSIUS	GAS
250	120	½	400	200	6
275	140	1	425	220	7
300	150	2	450	230	8
325	160	3	475	240	9
350	180	4	500	260	10
375	190	5			